JEAN MUS

MEDITERRANEAN GARDENS

DANE McDOWELL
PHOTOGRAPHS BY VINCENT MOTTE

Flammarion

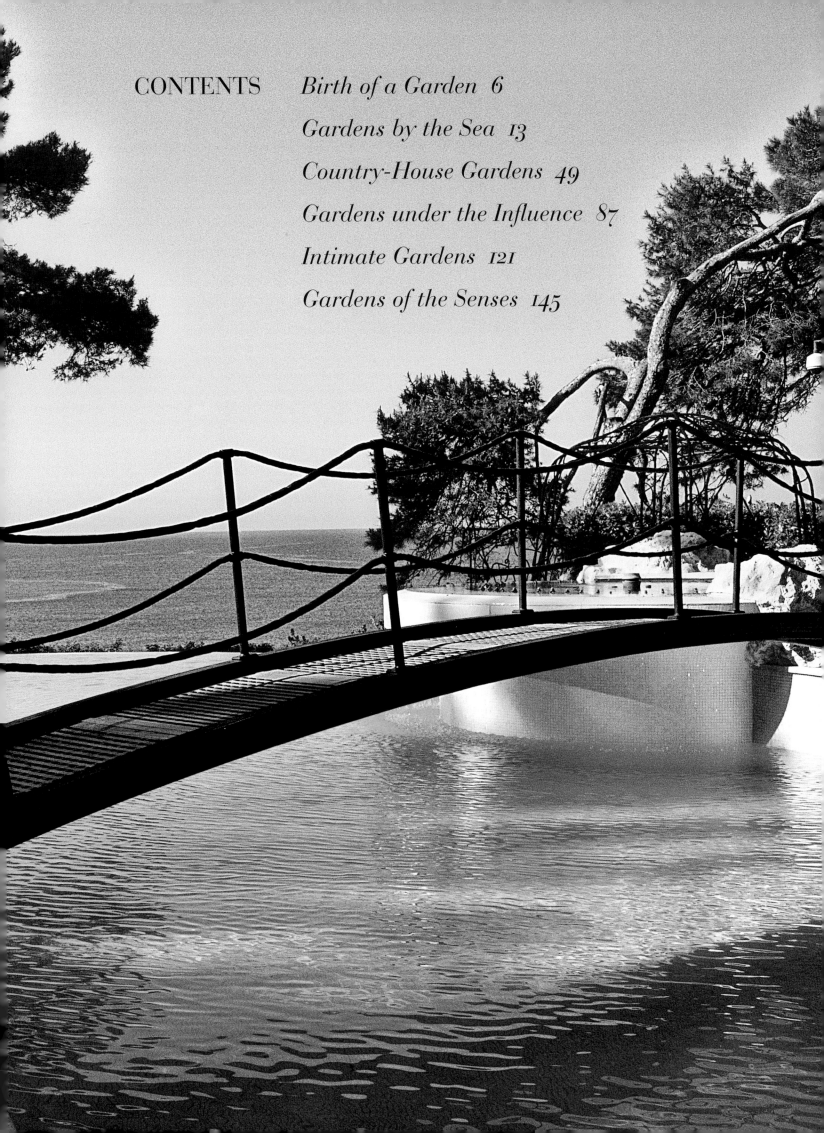

CONTENTS

The Birth of a Garden

Pages 2–3: Designed by Jean Mus, a wrought-iron banister in the shape of a creeper supports a star jasmine.
Pages 4–5: A footbridge made from tropical wood crosses an infinity pool.
Above: Plants can also have their own architecture, as, for example, these acanthus.
Facing page: The shepherd's refuge, or borie *in Provence, fits in perfectly with the range of native plants (immortelles, box, lavender, santolina, etc.).*

Whether perched above the Mediterranean or nestling in the heart of a town, whether inspired by rural tradition or by the history of Italy, Greece, and Portugal, or governed by a joyous sensuality, the gardens of Jean Mus show that imagination and sensitivity are more important than the ruler and the compass. In contrast to the cold and intellectual aesthetic of Le Nôtre, Jean Mus, a student of the École Nationale Supériéure du Paysage de Versailles (the National Institute of Landscape Design), prefers emotion. He is only partly satisfied with imposing order on nature, and although he is interested in the design of French-style gardens, he dreams of the fragrances of Provence. He answers the dictates of geometry with subtlety.

Returning after his studies to the region where he had grown up, Jean Mus followed in the footsteps of his father, who was head gardener at the Villa Croisset, created by the famous society garden designer, Ferdinand Bac. Jean Mus manages to incorporate into his own style the lessons he learned from Bac, without betraying the teachings of Le Nôtre. Like a theater designer, he refuses to reveal everything at the same time. He composes his gardens like a journey of initiation, playing with surprise effects and using a range of styles and inventions in which all techniques are allowed, provided they look good. "The garden," he declares "is the most beautiful kind of entertainment." If charm rather than grandeur is the order of the day, the layout is always rigorous. Thus design becomes delight, and a new vision of paradise is sketched out with olive and cypress trees. Taking its cue from topography, the architecture of this particularly personal theater underpins sensation. Working with nature rather than against it, Jean Mus adds to his repertoire the creative freedom of a poet and a painter, mixing this with his sensuality and his passion for music.

Let us join Jean Mus while he is creating a garden, a process which happens over the course of a series of meetings. For the project to be drawn up there has to be a rapport, a meeting of minds, between the landscape architect and the owners.

"During the initial visit to the site," says Jean Mus, "I rely on my instincts. While I take note of my own impressions, I listen to the clients to be able to translate their words into forms and imagine a garden that is a synthesis of their ideas and mine." The couple commissioning the design, reassured by Mus, talk about their preferences and their dreams. The next stage involves discussions with the professionals: "I like to talk to the architect first, as he has a rightful claim to look over the plans for the space. He wants his concept to be extended harmoniously to the outside. I involve the interior designer, whose tastes are usually attuned to that of the owners, in the general discussion. The gardener is the third person to be consulted, as it is his 'territory.' I also reassure the cook that he will have a *potager* for his vegetables, fruits, and herbs, especially if the owners of the house have busy social lives. But at the end of the day, it's me who retains control of the situation." In fact, the contract signed between the parties simply sets out the ground rules to be followed. The signing is always an emotional moment: one of Jean Mus's most cherished memories is when a client simply wrote at the bottom of the page, "Let's go!"

Fortunately, it is not just billionaires who have the passion to create a garden. Money is not the only motivation in this business, and the idea of pleasure does not have a price tag. "That's one of the reasons why I don't like to be given *carte blanche*," says Jean Mus. "Dialogue and the sharing of ideas are essential from the beginning to the end of this exciting adventure." In most cases, full and thorough discussion and serious debate lead to results. It is then time to move into action and to get started on the design, which begins with a pre-planning stage, comprising a master plan, photos, and samples. According to the designer, "It's a declaration of love for the future of the relationship between architect and client." The project is then finalized, and the plans are digitally rendered to facilitate rapid and efficient communication. They deal with the leveling of the site, the civil engineering, the lighting, the irrigation, and everything concerning the construction work, down to the metalwork. The planting list is added to these technical documents, so that expert suppliers can calculate the cost of the work. "When it comes to plants, I am most concerned by the architectural forms of the trees and by color, and less interested in the flowers. I stick to a discreet palette made up of blues, grays, and whites, to which I sometimes add a touch of something more colorful." The clients receive several computer renderings which have been colored by hand. "I refuse to let myself be bullied by a computer," says Jean Mus rebelliously. "Nothing beats the pencil or pen to share the emotion of a sketch."

Once the project is agreed, the great adventure can begin at last. Up until this point, nothing has happened on site. From now until the work is finished, there is a growing sense of anticipation. "With my assistants, who keep a journal of the works

Facing page: A reception courtyard in an Italianate garden, where an ancient fountain plays among lush vegetation.

where all the events are recorded, I visit the site twice a week, to keep an eye on the progress and to see my ideas take on concrete form." A day of practical work, a real trip to the country, is scheduled for the owners. "I like them to come with me when I go to the plant nursery to find the plants we've chosen. We put on our gardening clothes, pull on our boots, and find a nice little restaurant in the country where we can stop for lunch. Talking to the specialist who has grown the plants is a wonderful experience. The day continues with further visits to antique shops, potters, and architectural salvage dealers. The clients enjoy themselves, hoping to pick up some bargains and make new finds which they can use to enhance their decor."

Every site has its surprises and the architect must take stock of them calmly. For those who have never lived in the South of France, floods, drought, and even two days of rain are unacceptable, and someone has to take the blame. One learns to put up with the imperfections which are part of the charm and color of Mediterranean regions. Absolute priority must be given to the planting times. "Every self-respecting gardener works with the seasons and the phases of the moon, knowing that the plant will be the first to notice any tricks," insists Jean Mus. Finally, the long-awaited day of the handover to the client arrives: "We have brought a child into the world, a marvelous garden, and it's an emotional moment when this fragile and capricious landscape is given back to the owners. Will this creation, designed for eternity, prove to be ephemeral? The moment the garden is handed over is a real lesson in humility. When the owner allows me to speak about his property as 'our garden,' that makes me very happy—because I have succeeded in sharing my passion, and in communicating my close and special relationship with nature."

Jean Mus creates extraordinary gardens whose spirit reflects his love for the land that formed him, redrawing a map of the emotions with patience and wonder. Through a spectacular dialogue of shapes, colors, and fragrances, these twenty secret gardens—among hundreds of others—are acts of faith and hope which celebrate the good fortune of living on the shores of the Mediterranean. Jean Mus is an architect of gardens, but above all he is an architect of emotions.

Facing page: This patchwork of box and santolina illustrates the garden's masterly arrangement of volumes and colors.

Below: Jean Mus sometimes lets nature overrun the surroundings of the house, using climbing plants that he appears not to control.

GARDENS
BY THE SEA

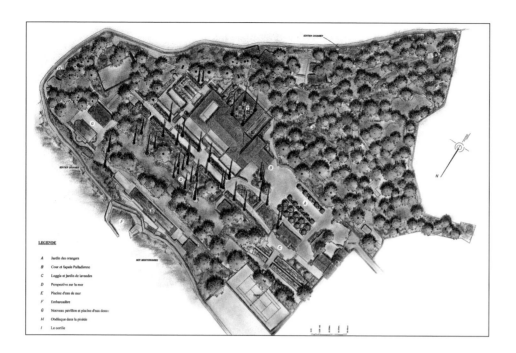

A Legendary Garden

Preceding pages: At Théoule, the sophisticated, wild garden tumbles into a beautiful Mediterranean inlet. Working within the limitations set by a rocky terrain, Jean Mus has skillfully tamed the Provençal maquis.
Above: The master plan of La Fiorentina shows clearly the Italian inspiration for the layout, and the very natural design, in keeping with the character of the landscape.
Facing page: "I introduce the exotic garden's cascade through a shady path where the water's musical notes can already be heard," Jean Mus explains. Tall Aleppo pines shade the playful cycas and the Destrelizia augusti folia. *A carpet of* Polygonum capitatum *adds softness.*

The villa Fiorentina is a place of myth and magic, belonging both to history and to the legendary past of the Côte d'Azur. The villa's past reads like an incomparably romantic novel and new chapters are still being added today, the most recent being the total rebuilding of the villa. The owners naturally entrusted Jean Mus with the restoration of the gardens.

He has fond memories of the collaboration: "This place was waiting for me. As the spiritual descendent of Ferdinand Bac, I know all his gardens intimately, every corner, every perspective, the very fabric of the gardens, the way the colors interact. I am an admirer of his watercolors, and I have read everything that he has written. I grew up at the Villa Croisset, so I have a great affinity with his work and feel a strong rapport with this exceptional designer."

The first owner of La Fiorentina, the Countess of Beauchamp, met Ferdinand Bac for the first time in 1917 during a visit to the Villa Croisset, where Bac was putting the finishing touches to the gardens. Around this time, Ferdinand Bac, a society figure turned landscape architect, spent long days and nights in the glittering surroundings of the Paris salons. The illegitimate grandson of the King of Westphalia, Jérôme Bonaparte, Bac had at last found his vocation: to design highly architectural gardens which emphasized Mediterranean flora and broke free from the Anglo-Saxon obsession with exotics and imported plants, which was all the rage along the Côte d'Azur. The garden at Villa Croisset was much admired by elegant society. Thérèse de Beauchamp was impressed by the talent of this socialite landscape gardener, and suggested to the then fifty-eight-year-old Bac that he transform her residence on the Côte d'Azur. Bac was immediately smitten by the beauty of La Fiorentina and shared his vision with the countess. Admiring the wind-tormented Aleppo pines and the rocks which he saw as "a pedestal hewn by continuous violence," he envisaged the summer residence of a cultivated and aesthetic clergyman, surrounded by three themed

gardens combining the notions of time and space. As at Villa Croisset, Bac recommended a red wash for the façade, a color which he had come across in the paintings of Carpaccio, and which perfectly complemented the green of the olive trees. Covered over by previous owners, the walls of La Fiorentina are Carpaccio-red once again.

"What I admire in Bac's gardens, such as those he created at La Fiorentina, are their audacity, their freedom, and the combination of lavish decor and quiet intimacy," says Jean Mus. "It is through him that I came to understand that beauty is to be found not in opulence, but in simplicity."

Roderick Cameron and Russell Page had given the villa an Anglo-Saxon aesthetic which was a little too restrained. True to his master, Ferdinand Bac, Jean Mus endeavored to give back some of its energy and drama. He designed the garden like a theater production, that reflected the philosophy and architecture of the house. The first act serves as an introduction and sets the tone. The second announces the plot and subplots, and after a *coup de théâtre* where the action reaches its climax, the last act reaches a happy ending. Here, the spectator witnesses a reconciliation and perhaps a realization of something new and different.

"I believe in first impressions," emphasizes Jean Mus. "I want people to think immediately of Mediterranean enchantment as soon as they see La Fiorentina. I left the tall pines to frame and emphasize the house, and I reintroduced the orange trees with their lime-washed trunks, just as Roderick Cameron had imagined them. I reworked the perspective of the cypress-lined, royal avenue, with its grass-covered, stone steps leading down to the sea, defining, as it always has done, the splendor of La Fiorentina. Incidentally, it was the English architect Harold Ainsworth Peto who laid it out before Ferdinand Bac's involvement." An element of mystery is introduced in act

Facing page, top: A burble of water from the fountain in the hexagonal pool refreshes the enclosed garden.
Facing page, bottom: Behind the fleshy leaves of Ligularia kaempferi, *a fountain hewn from tufa stone supports green festoons of helxine.*
Above, left: A decorative, Moorish arch serves as a backdrop to a canal, evoking the splendor of the gardens of the Alhambra. The walls have been adorned with Ficus repens *and star jasmine.*
Above, right: Pots on the main Italian terrace. Cushions of westringia echo the square, terra-cotta tiles.
Following pages: From the seawater swimming pool the great staircase, guarded by two sphinxes, climbs between a double row of Florentine cypresses and Buxus sempervirens *towards the palazzo.*

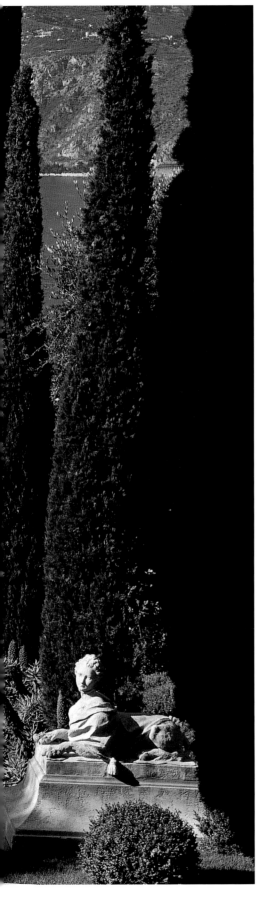

Left: *A broad sweep of Florentine cypresses leads majestically from the swimming pool toward the sea.*

Right: *A study in topiary in the shade of an Aleppo pine. The gardener has now become a sculptor, as he masters the double row of variegated spindle-trees (*Euonymus argentea*) and takes inspiration from the lines of this conifer.*

two, with a series of corridors, hallways, stairs, and green rooms, divided up by trimmed *Pittosporum tobira* hedges, which redraw nature and set the scene for romance. These green rooms break up the stunning views over the Mediterranean: by hiding the shimmering sea, Mus encourages the visitor to spend time discovering the beautiful trees and flowers, and to stop in front of the monumental statues silhouetted at the end of an avenue or in a clearing. Rodin's *Balzac* here, a sphere, obelisk or archway by Pomodoro there, each redefines the space around them. Roses, hibiscuses, and bougainvilleas provide a complete color spectrum of orange, ocher, crimson, vermilion, and purple, mirroring the Carpaccio red of the house set against the slate-blue sky. With a talent for aesthetics, the owner knew that these bright colors would convey perfectly the Mediterranean spirit of La Fiorentina. The colonnaded cloister has retained its saffron hue and its water channel, while the terrace, an extension of the south-facing living room, has been transformed into an elegant reception room, a place from which to view the magical spectacle of the waves dashing against the rocks.

The *coup de théâtre* and necessary climax of the third act, however, is a truly original creation by Jean Mus—a secret garden. Access is via a narrow path, wide enough for just one person at a time, bordered by bamboo which screens everything else from view. Emerging from this shady jungle, the visitor is startled by the light and the sound of a waterfall bursting forth from a cliff into a stretch of water amid a cluster of arborescent ferns and giant-leafed alocasia. The theme of a journey, which Ferdinand Bac adored, is skillfully taken up by Jean Mus who adds spice and a touch of the exotic by introducing the music and drama of tumbling water, the contrast of light and shade, and finally, a sense of mystery. This tropical garden is a link between the exotic gardens of the Belle Époque and contemporary gardens which often take their inspiration from the Orient. "This is an intimate place, slightly troubling, designed to inspire dreams and to encourage the exploration of nature, still wild but generous and benevolent. The abundance of succulent plants and luxuriant vegetation contrasts with the rocky shoreline and the stiffness of the pines."

Facing page, top: In the main courtyard, an orange-tree garden welcomes guests. The trees, contained within low, wooden surrounds, have had their trunks coated in limewash to deter insects, and to protect them from the heat.

Facing page, bottom: "You only need thirty years or so to achieve this sort of plant sculpture," jokes Jean Mus. "This woolly-looking Cupressus sempervirens pyramidalis *was a lesson in patience."*

*Above, right: Partly hidden by elephant ears (*Alocasia colocasia*), the Chinese parilion proudly wears the colors of the palazzo, evoking the workmanship of the gardens which have been designed on the theme of a journey.*

Undeniably the denouement is found at the highest point of the property, where a marble belvedere invites the visitor to discover one of the most beautiful views of the Côte d'Azur, and to view the real world from on high. The belvedere is an elegant reference to the ancient world and is the owner's favorite place. On one hand, he likes to survey his home from up here, and on the other hand, he never tires of the harmonious relationship between plants and rocks, which finds its true purpose overlooking the Mediterranean. This important and intimate place is reached by a steep path through the Provençal maquis or scrub. Jean Mus has reintroduced native flora—umbrella pines, laurels, and green oaks—and has lined the winding path with fragrant scrubland plants. He has chosen the plants with love and care, arranging them so that anyone walking by will be seduced and rewarded by their perfume.

"Like the buildings that adorned the parks in the eighteenth century and which Ferdinand Bac emphasized, the belvedere plays its part in the life of the garden," explains Jean Mus, "because it forces visitors to make a tour of the property, to move away from the well-marked paths and the structured green rooms, to lose any form of civilization in the garden for a few minutes. They will find themselves in the heart of a pine forest at the top of a hill where they can take stock of the panorama in their own way. It's a point of reference, a retreat to be shared only with close friends and family."

The gardens of La Fiorentina show garden design at its very best. Rarely has such harmony between design and planting reached such perfection, rarely has one place so completely captivated the eye, not just focusing on a single feature, but offering up a seemingly endless array of visual wonders, which complement each other in perfect logic, coherence, and harmony.

Wilderness Tamed

Above: A wall covered in star jasmine is the backdrop for a harmonious scattering of cushions of Pittosporum Nana *and* Strelizia reginae.
Facing page: "We have imitated nature," admits Jean Mus, "by installing rocks which support the ground, allowing the olive trees to grow toward the light. We have used eriocephalus, with its glorious gray hues, to carpet the ground. The little path which runs alongside the plantings has been paved with layered rock salvaged from the site."

In a prestigious residential enclave near Théoule, Jean Mus has created a garden perched above the sea, imbued with Mediterranean civilization in all its extremes, passions, and moods. The blood-red rock of the Esterel hills serves as a backdrop to the stones and plants of this area, bringing to mind the rugged paintings of the Fauvists. The rocks and sheer cliff act as anchors for the plants and the garden's outdoor structures. They define the boundaries of the property and divide it into intimate spaces which are carefully enclosed by low walls and cypress hedges.

Jean Mus knew that the house was going to be redesigned by Jean-Michel Wilmotte, a famous, demanding, and passionate architect, so he could not ignore the minimalist lines of the architecture or the harsh beauty of the place. He also had to respect the conditions imposed by the environment and the climate. Except for a few giant Lambert cypresses, their trunks beaten by the violent gusts of the mistral, the landscape was dominated by scrub, made up of sparse, perfumed plants. The owner had a certain idea in mind. He was particularly fond of the acclimatized gardens of the romantic Riviera, and his dream was for a garden full of exotic plants. He called on Jean Mus to create such a paradise. It was not easy, as Jean Mus explains: "More than anything else, I wanted to retain that sense of emotion which takes hold of you as you enter the garden for the first time. It was really a matter of leaving the wild and majestic look of nature and introducing tropical plants without making it too domesticated." Jean Mus did not discuss these issues with Wilmotte, yet he created a garden which looks as though it has been there for decades. Mindful of the need for harmony between buildings and plantings, he applied the principle of perspective to the location of the plants: for example, the topiary which surrounds the house becomes looser and freer as it moves from the house toward the sea, where it finally disappears.

"You have to know your friends and enemies," explains Mus. "If I can't tame the wind, and have to leave it to shape the plants by the sea, then, when I am working with extreme weather conditions, I put four protective shrubs in the front line of defense.

I use *Pittosporum, Limoniastrum,* tamarisks, and *Medicago arborea.* I have also put up woven Chinese bamboo to act as a shield and absorb the sea spray. It makes a natural and elegant barrier."

At the foot of the cliff, perched above the sea, is a free-form, double swimming pool. It is invisible from the house, so it has escaped the application of strict geometric lines. Three successive pools of more or less the same shade of blue merge into each other. Disoriented by the evocative power of the luxuriant plants, lulled by the gentle rustling of the palms, it is easy to imagine oneself on a beach in the Indian Ocean. "On the coast, I treat the exotic species as guests of honor. Here, for example, I have planted some chamaerops alongside tall date palms, and the effect is stunning," admits the man who quite simply loves Provence.

"I even felt as though I was in the sort of jungle 'Le Douanier' Rousseau would paint." Very near the main entrance, Jean Mus has used the geometric lines of the space to blend with Wilmotte's rectilinear architecture. Using the perpendicular nature of the rocks, he has created a waterfall, a simple, vertical feature dug into the cliff. From there, he has plotted a T-shaped water channel which leads to a seawater swimming pool, sculpted into the rock, creating a logical and seamless transition from mountain to sea.

"My work as a landscape architect has consisted mainly of framing some of the most spectacular views. Here, of course, that means the gaps through which the sea is glimpsed. Getting the right perspective was a huge challenge in this uneven, hilly, and rocky landscape," explains Mus. "Not having vast spaces to work with meant I only had the element of surprise or even wonder to play with, so I varied the rhythm by adding interludes, rests, and pauses as in a musical score." Varying the height and breadth of the plants, he arranged them in groups, sometimes planting them vertically with a row of Provençal cypresses acting as a wall, and sometimes horizontally, with clusters of *Pistacia lentiscus* trimmed very low, and globes of dwarf pittosporum, their curves emphasizing the right-angled lines.

The sole survivors from the former garden are the celebrated Lambert cypresses. They stand tall and proud above the palms and Aleppo pines and continue to offer protection to the exotic plants. Linking the tropical paradise to the topiary garden, interlacing steps hewn from the layered rock mark out passages across the property and lead visitors into the middle of two green rooms.

"The paths and steps connect the different levels in the garden, pacing the visitor on his journey. The steps are all eleven centimeters high and the stairs are laid out and positioned so that, wherever you stop, you get a different view," explains Jean Mus.

Facing page, top: With the Mediterranean as a backdrop, Aleppo pines overlooking a field of lavender stand out against the horizon, while in the foreground are Lantana selloviana.

Facing page, bottom: The Esterel rocks, clad in native plants including rosemary, myrtle, cistus, pittosporum, and Lantana delicatissima.

Above: Date palms reflected in a pool designed by Jean Mus. In the background, a curtain of mimosas and strawberry trees (Arbutus unedo) *gives bathers privacy.*

Following pages: Conscious of the rectilinear architecture of the house, Jean Mus has designed a canal and geometric pool which bring out the color of the plants and show them to their best advantage.

Inspired by the Provençal "tèse," a fence made of leaves and placed in the shade, originally used for ensnaring birds, the two plant rooms are ideal places to read or to share secrets. They are furnished with cane chairs, which are light and easy to move, and accord well with the rest of the garden.

Jean Mus is known for his harmonious use of white, blue, and gray, but the red rock of the Esterel hills plunging sheer into the deep blue of the Mediterranean seemed to demand more color, so Mus added vibrant hues to various parts of the garden. Now oleander, hibiscus, helichrysum, *Lantana camara*, tamarisk, and bird-of-paradise all burst into bloom at the first sign of spring. And Mus has certainly not forgotten his favorite tree, the olive. Positioned carefully, it blends seamlessly into the maritime landscape. Orange trees, lemon trees, night-blooming jasmine, sarcococca and star jasmine round off his perfumed palette of Mediterranean shrubs.

Fragrance enhances the whole garden. It is an important ingredient in Jean Mus's designs and he arranges it as though it were an invisible form of architecture. The magic of a place is not always obvious, and here, tamed by a master, the leading roles go to nature, to a reinvented form of exoticism, to poetic exuberance, and to a sensuality painted with a touch as light as a sea breeze imbued with the sweet fragrance of jasmine.

Facing page: These steps, wending their way through clumps of Pittosporum tobira nana, *are a key element in the clean, strong, and efficient architecture. The choice of stones is very important.*

Above, left: Built from rocks salvaged on site, a waterfall fits perfectly into this rugged environment. The sound of water tumbling over stones adds a touch of music to the garden.

Above, right: A gentle flight of stone steps built into a Bermuda-grass lawn. The dense leaves of the pittosporum, trimmed into round globes, absorb the salt from the sea.

A Garden of Light and Shade

Above: A subtle harmony is at play between the blue of the swimming pool and the blue of the sea. The branches of the Aleppo pines, molded by the wind, are reflected in the glass-like water.

Facing page: *The river pebbles which cover the steps have been carefully sized and laid, allowing people to walk barefoot down to the swimming pool.*

Protected by double rows of walls and cypresses, the magnificent houses of Cap d'Antibes will remain forever undiscovered, revealing the treasures and enchanted landscape they hide only to a privileged few. Through the half-open gate to one of these residences, however, you catch a glimpse of paradise—a paradise bearing the signature of Jean Mus. "This is a garden where light and shade play an important role," he explains. "One reveals the other. You have to walk through shade to earn the view that follows. This common approach, leading away from the property, was designed as a journey of initiation and is a reference to the great work of the alchemists who, to achieve their goal of turning lead into gold, had first to work in darkness."

The visitor, surprised by the contrast between the narrowness of the approach and the far-reaching panorama which unfolds beneath his gaze, stops for a few minutes to catch his breath. Before him, a wide area of lawn is divided by an avenue leading up to a fountain, framed by a semicircle of Greek columns. The visitor's progress is arrested by the beauty of the stone sculpture of Venus bathing in the fountain. He hesitates, not knowing which direction to take. To the right, hidden by sweet bay trees, giant pittosporum, bamboo, and pines, a sandy path leads to a small, wooden bridge, nestling between date palms and cycads. Its elegant curve spans a pond where arborescent ferns and water lilies have made their home. Continuing on his way, the visitor passes in front of a gracious, wrought-iron aviary and finds himself in the middle of a clearing surrounded by majestic Aleppo pines.

The comfortable chairs from the summer room, arranged beneath a white canopy, will offer him an opportunity to relax and admire the romantic fountain, tucked away in the greenery before him. If the visitor has chosen the path to the left, however, he heads towards the main house. The long, winding, and shaded avenue is lined with Mediterranean shrubs with dense foliage, and trees with their lower branches removed. It could easily be a scene from a fairy tale by Charles Perrault, a

*Left: An elegant gazebo
overlooking the Mediterranean is
an inviting place for conversation.
In the middle, a fountain is
encased by a circular bench
of Carrara marble.*
*Right: Alongside a belvedere,
cushions of* Pittosporum tobira
nana, *planted at various levels,
are strewn across the lawn.
Ever the pragmatist, Jean Mus
adds: "We leave the dead branches
on the pine trees, so that when
it's windy, they absorb the salt
of the sea spray."*

seventeenth-century, French children's writer, but thanks to Jean Mus, there are no thorns to trouble Prince Charming. At ground level, the avenue is punctuated by coleus, and pink and red impatiens, while flower-shaped lamps, designed by the architect, lend it rhythm. As the avenue approaches the coast, more light filters through, but not enough to reveal everything. By the time it reaches the entrance to the house, it skirts two enormous Canary pines and ends up as a pebble path outside one of the wings of the property.

On the subject of the pebble path, Jean Mus's eyes light up: "I asked the owner to remove her shoes and to walk barefoot on the round pebbles which had been selected and laid one by one by my team. Now she performs the same experiment on her own guests, asking them to remove their shoes. Of course, if just one pebble had shown any sign of roughness, we would have started all over again!"

Facing due south, the rear façade of the house extends onto a spacious terrace which has been transformed into a reception room. The red and orange roses in pots echo the ocher tones of the villa. Elegant wicker chairs are arranged as if in a box in the theater. The horizontal stone balustrade, covered in garlands of plumbago, lantana, and white-star jasmine, defines and frames the magical panorama. Lovers in search of a place to share confidences are safe here beneath the wrought-iron gazebo,

Facing page: A mosaic of river pebbles follows the curve of a terrace overlooking the sea.
Above: A Balinese hut beneath a Canary Island date palm adds a touch of the exotic.
Right: The flights of steps are carefully paced, creating pleasant and easy links in the steep parts of the garden.

in the middle of which a marble fountain's joyful, crystalline notes render their whispered declarations of love inaudible.

This idyllic scene may be bathed in the azure light of the Mediterranean, but the most spectacular part of the garden is still to come. Jean Mus has designed a handrail which leads down to the sea. Wrought in iron by a master craftsman, a supple vine serves as a support guiding the visitor into a perfumed labyrinth where dipladenia, cistus, and rosemary burst forth, despite the tapered tips of the aloes which pierce their many blooms.

"The sea tends to weaken plants," continues Jean Mus. "Planting must be carried out in spring so that the plants can adapt. If they are spared the wind and the salty, winter blasts then their leaves and wood can toughen up and ripen. My secret is to

Far left: A stipe resembles a stroke of calligraphy, next to the pointed leaves of a date palm.

Left: A dolphin sculpture leaps over a sea of Rhus typhina.

Far left, below: Perched on a carpet of Vittadinia, bronze egrets watch for fish. Beyond, a Japanese-inspired bridge spans the pond.

Facing page: Collections of seaside plants flank the steps leading to the swimming pool.

water well in the first year, then keep an eye on the soil conditions. When you can, wash down the leaves after they have been blasted by the sea."

At every turn and at every step inlaid with a pattern of pebbles, the visitor stops to take in the panorama opening up in front of him. In the presence of this eternal landscape, indelibly imprinted in his memory, the visitor stands silent, in quiet contemplation of the scene before him. When the sky is clear, the Saint-Tropez peninsula can be seen to the west, and the mountains of Corsica to the south. Below, sloops, schooners, and luxury yachts cross back and forth, leaving white wakes in the blue sea.

Facing out to sea, wrought-iron furniture creates a sophisticated salon. As the day draws to a close, the owner and his guests head for the armchairs strewn with brightly colored cushions and a gazebo covered in white gauze, to watch the sun set. Designed by Jean Mus, the rounded curves of the furniture are projected onto the fabric like calligraphic shadows. In this natural and elegant setting, where the plants assume an exotic charm, thoughts turn to the voluptuous poems of Omar Khayyám, which speak of life's joys and the pleasures of the senses. Enjoying the same view, a swimming pool nestles in the side of the rocks. Its sapphire-blue water echoes the deep blue of the Mediterranean and carries a message of purity and well-being. Thanks to Jean Mus, this garden has become a place of poetic inspiration. The impressive outline of a sculpture by a leading contemporary artist seems perfectly placed between the sea and the tropical flowers. The trees, foliage, and paths, and below, the glistening monochrome in blue, all act, as the author Michel Baridon describes in his book, *Les Jardins, paysagistes, jardiniers, poètes,* "like silent presences which accompany the visitor and seem to tell him that the artistic world can be understood only when these presences surround him." And it is perhaps at precisely this moment that the visitor realizes that the lead weight on his heart has just turned to gold.

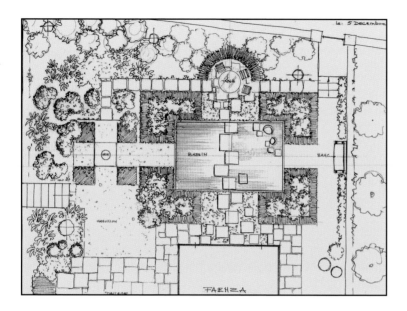

Green Rooms

In the heart of prestigious Cap d'Antibes, the great homes built at the end of the nineteenth century usually display some original feature as a clue to their past. It is not unusual to see the crenellated towers of a Gothic castle peeping out over the tops of umbrella pines, or the pink pediment of a Florentine palace. The parkland which surrounds these magnificent residences, however, in spite of dating from the same period, rarely gives any clue to their original layout. Not far from the Eden Roc hotel, considered the best in the area, is a good example of this. The exterior architecture of the houses which are part of this estate may have undergone only slight modifications, but the gardens have been completely changed at the express request of the owner. A great admirer of modern and contemporary art, he wanted to use his garden as a showcase for his collection. In partnership with Jean Mus, he gave free rein to the landscape architect, who began to ponder the task. "I had admired the work of an Italian interior designer, a young woman keen on minimalism, and I decided to apply this design philosophy throughout the garden. I asked myself what the definition of minimalism was. Of course, I was familiar with the phrase by the architect, Ludwig Mies van der Rohe, that 'less is more,' but you have to be careful not to limit your responses to notions of constraint and restriction alone. When you reduce the number of ideas, what's left must be truly excellent in order to create something unique and coherent." The purity of clear and fluid lines, open geometric shapes, and the absence of bright colors create an impression of calm, simplicity, and modernity. Unlike gardens designed in the early twentieth century, which were accumulations of disorder, easy theatricality, and superfluous ornament, this philosophy represents a break with tradition and, with its energetic and modern approach, a new beginning.

The garden, which sits on uneven land and whose extremity overlooks the Mediterranean, has been completely redesigned and re-laid to emphasize the beauty of the landscape and to create an atmosphere suited to quiet meditation. Jean Mus

Facing page, top: Under a white mulberry, cylindrical, earthenware vases give rhythm to the garden, while box, clipped into hedges and globes, juxtapose with the Burgundy-stone paving.
Facing page, bottom: With an eye to geometry, rectangular flagstones are placed across a pool overgrown with water lilies.
Right: A border of lavender follows the curve of a path.
Below: In the shade of a wall, decked in bougainvillea, a pond planted with Melianthus major *signals the entrance to the guests' house.*

began by redirecting the main avenue leading up to the house. He designed a path paved with hand-cut, white stones from Portugal which incorporated a fiber-optic system to create a truly magical lighting effect. This white path winds along an avenue packed tight with hundreds of swaying lavender bushes, protected by clusters of feijoa, lentisks, and eleagnus. Trimmed to follow the curve of the hill, the groups of plants work in harmony, the texture and color of their leaves contrasting with each other. "The gardener must also be a sculptor," remarks Jean Mus. "Clean shapes and lines are found throughout the property. In the same way that the Japanese observe the principle of *ma*, I have paid careful attention to the space between the plants, paths, stone structures, and art works. You have to find a balance between the size and spacing which allows both a visual and emotional response."

His appreciation of native plants led him to notice some magnificent *blanquetier* olive trees, a variety peculiar to Cap d'Antibes, and he immediately gave them prominence. The roughness of their ancient trunks contrasts sharply with the velvety green lawn, a contrast no visitor can fail to notice. A little further on is a group of giant birds-of-paradise, their spear-shaped leaves framing a breathtaking view of the Mediterranean.

Exoticism is everywhere, made more apparent still by a group of succulents, their statuesque silhouettes standing out against a Klein-blue sea. In front of the main villa, which has been modernized by the Italian interior designer Ivana Porfiri, a clearing surrounded by umbrella pines hides an oblong swimming pool, the water of which laps against the lawn. The rectilinear design of the swimming pool fits

well with the controlled organization of the land-scape. Skirting the house is a bamboo grove and beyond its flexible stalks a row of private, green rooms which, in turn, connects with the owners' private apartments. The delicate placement of a branch of umbrella pine frames a dream-like view that Signac, the nineteenth-century French pointillist painter, would certainly have wished to paint. Standing out against the dark green of the pine needles, the intense blue of the sea, barely disturbed by the white sails of a frigate, streaks across the horizon.

A decked terrace adjoining the rear façade of the house emphasizes the new geometry; a double avenue of orange trees, their trunks whitewashed with lime, extend the lines. From this same spot flows a water channel which one meets again lower down. At each level, the water divides into a number of geometric pools where brightly colored koi carp twist and turn between the water lilies. At the top, a *Magnolia grandiflora* offers its shade as protection for the carefully trimmed globes of box, while at the bottom the visitor is inclined to pause for a moment in this pastoral space, paved with round pebbles laid in the traditional, Provençal *calade* design. Wooden armchairs made to look like the trunks of trees are overgrown with Virginia creeper. Steps covered in vittadinia and set out at an attractive angle lead down to the lower part of the garden and invite the visitor to discover small, geometric gardens which surround the guests' villa. Here can be found an Italian-style garden surrounded by small, rectangular pools edged with beds of box, trimmed into T-shapes, while further on is a simple avenue lined with hedges of star jasmine, sage, and lantana, home to the statue of a Greek goddess.

"I did not allow strict geometric rules to govern me," comments Mus. "It was more about letting the beauty of the places and the lay of the land guide my work. True, I wanted to incorporate some aspects of modernism, but above all, I wanted to give free expression to the clean lines by using a minimum of plants in order to set off the architecture."

At Cap d'Antibes, nature has taught Jean Mus to think big, to dare, to work with native plants, and to skillfully reinterpret the Mediterranean landscape to create something as sculpted as Land Art. And the visitor, in an emotional response to the profundity and evocative quality of nature, finally understands that a garden can convey a message that is both cosmic and spiritual.

Preceding pages: Along the villa's graceful arcades, Jean Mus has planted a collection of brightly colored Chinese hibiscus which flower throughout the summer. Acting as a backdrop, Bougainvillea glabra *and* sanderiana, *and false jasmine add a tropical note, which suits this part of the garden.*

Facing page: In the foreground, Cassia corymbosa *is a welcome addition to the well-designed orange tree garden. The citrus trees sit in rectangular wells cut into the ground, which protect the trees from being over-watered and the area around the base of the trunks from being trampled.*

*Above: The flowering of the birds-of-paradise (*Strelitzia*) from January through June remains a source of wonder. Beside them, Barbary figs (*Opuntias, *or Indian figs) raise their sculptural forms. These two species thrive by the sea, provided they are in well-drained soil.*

COUNTRY-
HOUSE
GARDENS

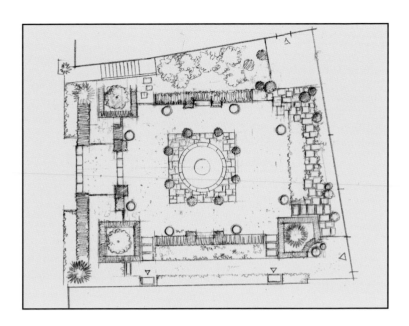

Cypress Country

Preceding pages: A row of terra cotta pots, arranged in an orderly line on a flight of steps, overlook a field bordered with olive trees and cypresses.
Above: Sketch of the main courtyard with imposing cypress trees in each of the four corners.
Facing page: This courtyard brings to the Grasse region the elegant formality of the bastides of Aix-en-Provence.

In the countryside surrounding Grasse, certain properties have not forgotten the Roman occupation, when Provence was still called Provincia. This is the case of the Vignal estate which still retains a fragment of a Roman road. Over the centuries, a *bastide* (a Provençal country house), replaced an old coach house and the vines grew to cover it, which gave it its name, Vignal, from *vigne*, the French word for vine. The present-day owners of Vignal wanted to keep with tradition and preserve its personality, closer in many ways to the hills around Aix-en-Provence than those behind Nice. They turned to Jean Mus, landscape designer and native of the region, to restructure their grounds.

"Of course, we kept the magnificent drive of plane trees which leads to the *bastide*. With its majestic wrought-iron gates decorated with vine leaves, it's a classic entrance which makes a reference to Aix-style gardens. I added two parallel rows of box trees pruned into spheres to add a touch of sophistication to the lawn, which retains a certain rustic poetry. This simple approach blends in with the typical architecture of the *bastide*, which was built in a horseshoe shape."

Several Provençal cypresses stand out in front of the façade of the *bastide*, which is covered in a layer of Persian ivy. To either side of the central staircase punctuated by pots from Biot, a nearby village renowned for its craftsmen, lavenders, rosemary, and agapanthus make up a palette of pastel colors. Slightly set back, the main courtyard with its central fountain welcomes guests and, on the days when the mistral blows, is transformed into a summer dining room well protected from the breeze. Accentuated by yew trees shaped into cones in the Italian style, the elegant stone balustrade which borders the rear terrace evokes the charm of the *bastides* of eastern Provence. Facing due south, the terrace offers a magnificent view over the countryside, framed on one side by the fortified village of Châteauneuf and on the other by the town of Grasse.

"A field of lavender, curtains of cypresses interspersed with olive trees, a view over the surrounding villages … the design spoke for itself," explains Jean Mus modestly.

Below: Forming a canopy the plane trees of the main avenue accompany the visitor's footsteps. The big spheres of box soften the vertical lines of these hundred-year-old trees.

Top, left: A hedge of pyramid-shaped cypresses (three per linear yard) form a supple and natural hedge.
Top, right: Candle-shaped cypresses give rhythm to the landscape.
Above: Surrounding the swimming pool, bamboo and draecena revive an exoticism already in vogue in the nineteenth century.

52

Right: *Behind an Anduze vase, topiaried santolinas sit next to a box hedge. Between two cypress trees, Japanese nandinia flower against the wall of the* bastide.

"In this garden, space is given priority over plants. Two hectares so close to the shores of the Mediterranean are rare indeed. I had to choose trees and shrubs carefully and highlight the idea of the greater landscape. I needed the vertical lines of the cypresses to frame it. I like their watchful stance which acts as a landmark," he comments.

Below the terrace, the owners wanted their swimming pool to be surrounded by a tropical garden. Bamboo, phormiums, and dwarf palms create an oasis in the eighteenth-century style, a time of passionate interest in exoticism and chinoiserie.

Leaving this area of acclimatized plants, the visitor descends to the lower part of the garden to find the last vestiges of the Roman road. A small waterfall borders the ancient route and serves as a boundary with the edge of the forest of white oaks which surround the property. This partly wild corner of the garden reflects a desire to preserve the historic past of the property. The gardeners cleared this area but respected the course of the paths lined with fruit trees, which monks from Lérins abbey used in the Middle Ages when they came to make their retreats.

Jean Mus rediscovered the language of childhood to evoke the pleasures of walking and foraging for food. "Did you know," he asks, "that the white oak was the original tree in the Provençal forest? Today it punctuates the walks along these free-form green avenues." And he points out a Judas tree and a copse of hazels which would appeal to a small family of squirrels. He pauses by some wild blackberry bushes, not minding that the juicy berries stain his hands. He talks also about Cade juniper, *Juniper oxyacanta*, the favorite conifer of the thrushes and blackbirds of

Provence and, a few meters further on, about the rowan tree whose fruits can be used to make a brandy much prized by the local people. Nature and her many bounties are also apparent on the path back to the *bastide*.

"Here at Vignal, each month brings its own delightful tastes. At the end of April," continues Jean Mus, pointing out the fruit trees, "the cherry trees with their white blossoms will stand out between the dark verticals of the cypresses. In the moist parts of the garden, the Belone fig trees will fill the fruit baskets for a good two months in the summer. In the gray days of December, the persimmons will light up the countryside with their sunny lanterns."

Finally a collection of local grape varieties: servan, clairette, and muscat, have been planted on a small hillside as a reminder of the property's origins. Near to a wine cellar, which adjoins the keepers' house, a stone fountain dating from the eighteenth century, invites you to refresh your hands in its cool water and to pause to admire the wine storehouse, restored down to the last detail using local materials. The Vignal estate is a perfect example of the conservation of agricultural heritage, one of the missions of the garden's designer. Have the owners achieved their aims? "Most definitely," they acknowledge. "Our first priority was to give Vignal its identity back. But the second was to enjoy ourselves and to experience the happiness of living in the south of France, to greedily savor each minute of it."

Preceding pages: At the sides of the main avenue, the vertical lines of the cypress alternate with the oblique lines of the Aleppo pines.
Facing page: Longer-lasting than the hemerocallis in the foreground, the blue flowers of the perovskia continue to bloom all summer above the cushions of the dwarf pittosporum.
Above: Sometimes the rough planting escapes the boundaries of a walk.

A Shepherd's Retreat in the Hills

Above: *In the new part of the property, a field of lavender has been introduced between newly planted, hundred-year-old olive trees.*
Facing page: *The classic* calade, *or Provençal paving, made with stones found on site, is accompanied by indigenous plants: germanders, gray santolinas and prostrate rosemary are planted in layers below a dragon tree.*

The countryside around Saint-Paul-de-Vence holds many surprises. Close to residential areas where superb Hollywood-style villas sprawl, some rare hills have succeeded in preserving their traditional look. On one of them is a sheep farm, built more than two hundred years ago with stone from a local quarry, hidden in the middle of a forest of green oaks. It is precisely this bucolic charm, far from the regimented villages of the Côte d'Azur, which attracted its owners. Provence and the Côte d'Azur owe much to the English who, more than the French, have the taste and respect for tradition and who consider horticulture a noble activity. Not wanting a Californian-style garden, they called in Jean Mus almost ten years ago, to translate their wishes into a pastoral landscape and to bring back to life, with a hint of nostalgia, the rural existence so battered by urban civilization. In spite of this, they wanted to have the benefit of a swimming pool and a tennis court, but these new structures had to blend into the vegetation and not draw attention to themselves.

"It wasn't so much a game of hide-and-seek as a reflection on the special connections between nature and architecture," explains the landscape designer. "From the start I loved the poetry of the old sheepfold and I accepted this job as challenge from which I could learn valuable lessons. An English architect, Robert Dallas, restored the old building to make it habitable and slightly more sophisticated. As for me, I got on with the exteriors with a certain spring in my step."

In front of the house the green oak forest dominates the scene. Winding through the trees and around a majestic dragon tree, a pavement of irregular rectangular stones fans out in front of the entrance. Just opposite the door, Jean Mus pictured a scene of rustic vegetation using box plants and rejected any notion of symmetry: "I wanted to give the impression that nature had hardly been disturbed by the hand of man." Unaware of the British love of mixed borders in rainbow colors, Jean Mus preferred to limit his choice to shades of green. This decision is carried

Left: *"Happiness is in the field"—which is allowed to go yellow in the summer, but which is always bright thanks to the lavender which flowers from June to July. The lavender must be cut before August.*
Right: *The palette of gray, blue, and green is combined with a roof of brick-colored tiles, weathered over time. The roof supports a population of saxicoline plants: umbilicus and sedum.*

through as you go around the house taking a path covered in crazy paving, to arrive in front of the rear façade.

"To make the owners happy, I planted sage, scented geraniums, and abitulons with purple flowers, but I kept the country charm of the old sheepfold," confides Jean Mus. The old building which was used as a sheep pen, has become a delightful outdoor kitchen, opposite which a small stone pond holds flowering water lilies. Concealed by olive and mandarin trees at the feet of which ivies and large-leaved ligularias grow, the swimming pool is strictly private, as is the tennis court, which is hidden from view and set further down the hill. It is a remarkable demonstration of the use of vegetation as camouflage. However, a mysterious stone staircase covered in moss invites the visitor to discover the secrets of these sporting retreats. Another surprise awaits the visitor as he strolls along the path: the old sheepfold has recently been attached to another, newer, property, which Robert Dallas has patiently restored. "I had to make a coherent transition between these two buildings, so I extended the stone path of the old sheepfold and took advantage of the area where the oak forest is more thinly planted. I discovered centuries' old fruit trees, including a fig tree, a smoke tree, and numerous olive trees," recounts Jean Mus. The presence of Provençal civilization is heightened the closer one gets to the new shepherd's house framed by the dark silhouettes of the cypresses. In a more ordered landscape, rosebushes, iris, rosemary, lavender cottons, valerians, and a collection of cistus and germanders punctuate the dry-stone wall with colors dear to Jean Mus, shades of gray, pink, and blue. Will the visitor have an eye for these delicate flowerings if he ventures into the clearing situated above the house? Under a dozen olive trees, the lavender bushes play with light and shade. It might look like a picture-postcard landscape, but this pastoral idyll corresponds to an idea of beauty etched into the deepest recesses of our unconscious minds, a Platonic image, moreover, because what is beautiful is also good.

An Epicurean's Mill

Near the village of Châteauneuf-de-Grasse, an ancient oil mill has, for what seems like forever, overlooked terraces planted with olive trees. Now, thanks to the efforts of its owners, it has found its true purpose again. Over the centuries, the miller's house has been transformed into an adorable pink *bastide* with blue shutters. Passionate about art and horticulture, the owners dreamed of a garden worthy of their new house. They entrusted Jean Mus with the task of creating it, a mission he accomplished so well that two years later the garden was awarded an "Arbre d'or," the highest distinction for a landscape architect. "For my part," Mus says, "I wanted the owners, who have become dear friends, to love Provence. At the time, there was a gardening culture on the Côte d'Azur which differed from that of Provence, but we found common cause in a daily passion for the garden as it is."

Protected by stone walls which form a rampart, the entrance gives away nothing about the beauty to come. As round as the millstone itself, a fountain takes pride of place in the main courtyard, shaded by venerable olive trees and paved with ancient stones. It is only by walking round the house that the size and the beauty of the garden become apparent. Judging by the size of the trees and the luxuriance of the plants, the trees, and the copses, one would swear that this garden, which is in reality only a few years old, had existed forever. In fact, the layout of the garden has been orchestrated by the hand of a master following a discreet and distinctive geometry.

The terraces that surround the house provide a wonderful transition between architecture and nature. In the spring, an arbor overrun by the mauve, silky flowers of wisteria is the star attraction of the garden. In summer, it is two giant plane trees which preside over lunches and dinners. On the lowest branches the mistress of the house hangs lanterns, and the atmosphere becomes magical at sunset when the countryside is bathed in violet and purple light. "It's here that everything began,

Above, left: An arbor made from woven bamboo shades a wooden bench. In the foreground, cottony cistus adds a touch of flirtatiousness in April and May.
Above, right: The large embankment which towers over the swimming pool is supported by rocks found on the hill and then carefully arranged to imitate nature.
Right: Following a favorite perspective of Jean Mus, a linear canal underlines the length of the stone-walled terrace. In the background, a bronze circle by Bruno Romeda draws the eye.

around the stone table," recounts the owner. "I urged Jean Mus, even forced him to design this garden. I also asked him to use flowers to add color."

"My task wasn't so simple," the architect replies. "I had to find a rational and harmonious way to connect the olive grove to the more ordered parts of the garden. The presence of flowers, as well as that of statues, must look natural nor forced. So I suggested a selection of architectural flowers, climbing roses, irises, *Choysia ternata*, lavender cottons, groundsel cineraria, agapanthus, and their complement, lavender pruned into balls, to keep the olive trees company." From the summer dining room, guests can admire the statue of a bronze dancer who appears to be leaping above the horizon. Hidden by clumps of immortelles and rosemary, several surprises are in store for the visitor at the first level of the stone terraces. Located directly in front of the house, a bucolic scene seems to step straight out of a painting by Fragonard, another famous son of Grasse. Are these stone shepherds, looking at a simple plank of wood suspended from the branch of an olive tree, dreaming of taking flight on a swing adorned with ribbons? Just next to this statue, concealed behind cascades of Lady Banks roses, a romantic garden hides a pool overgrown with rushes and cattails, where a flute player is charming a shoal of Japanese carp.

On the other side, the swimming pool, a simple rectangular basin, reflects the color of the sky. But the surprises do not end with this serene, minimalist vision. The visitor's gaze is drawn by a bronze circle by the artist Bruno Romeda. This masterpiece serves as a frame for another garden below: at the far end of a narrow pond, a monumental sculpture by Mimmo Palladino, displayed like a modern jewel on a lawn, completes the picture. The lowest part of the garden is just as wooded and is

set aside for the games for children of all ages. Under the children's teahouse, a mini-golf course jostles for space with an area for playing boules.

Although the geometry is discreet, it does make its presence felt. The horizontal alignment of the stone-walled terraces is countered by two vertical lines, stone staircases punctuated by cypress and shaded by an arbor of Lady Banks roses. On both sides four hundred olive trees jealously share the ground with rows of lavender. The olive harvest, which takes place between the end of November and the end of January, is accompanied by colorful and happy celebrations. The olives are transported to nearby Opio and shortly afterwards are transformed into five hundred liters of a beautiful amber-colored oil which will delight gourmet friends.

Halfway along the path, romantically inclined visitors can leave the steps to take refuge in the intimacy of a wrought-iron arbor weighed down with roses. This sublime viewpoint over the rolling hills of the countryside, ideal for meetings and confidences, recalls the wisdom of Provençal peasants who knew how to distill every instant to fix it forever in their memory. Jean Mus quotes his favorite proverb: "If you don't know the smell of the earth or which way the wind is blowing, you are the poorest man in the world."

The mill garden offers nourishment to the body and to the soul: it speaks directly using a series of images, of fleeting fragrances and tender colors, of happiness on earth.

Facing page, top: Transformed into a pond, the former swimming pool welcomes a flute player who is trying to charm the stone figures. Without losing an ounce of its elegance, the disheveled vegetation blends well with the informal but refined atmosphere of this part of the garden.

Facing page, bottom: Fed by a natural spring, a basin in the shape of a washtub refreshes the hands of visitors and can also hold a few good bottles of Provençal rosé at mealtimes.

Above, left: A flight of winding steps, discreet and easy to use, leads sportier guests to the swimming pool.

Above, right: A small stone-flagged path makes its way through a field of lavender to reach the area for playing boules.

The Cloister Garden

Above: *In this drawing by Jean Mus, the cypresses determine the vanishing point of the grand, Italian-style perspective.*

Facing page: *The ancient layout of the box has been scrupulously respected by Jean Mus. The gardener will take charge of maintaining the proportions of the box shapes, with the help of a gardener's line, shears, and secateurs.*

Dominating a green hill at the foot of Vence, a *bastide* with pink walls stands proud under the benevolent protection of green oaks and huge Aleppo pines. Their tops tower over the stone walls, but once the wrought-iron gate has been pushed open, an atmosphere of well-being awaits. The owners entrusted Jean Mus with the restoration of the gardens, and with great pleasure he took on the project. Built at the beginning of the twentieth century, this pretty house and its garden had a history. "They asked me to restore the former style of the place and to imagine a contemporary garden which brings out the exceptional location of the property."

The beauty, size, and positioning of the trees is explained by the history of the house, which belonged to a family of grain merchants, as famous for their hard work as for their refinement. It is a garden of the senses, without being an English garden. Geometry is present, but it is softened by the importance given to the natural landscape. Jean Mus remembered well the lessons learned from Capability Brown, but he did not abandon either the gardener's line, or the spirit level, or the beautiful perspectives. "What I like about the work of that great British landscape gardener, is that he was one of the first to realize that the garden plays on the emotions as much as on the senses."

The visitor approaches the house by taking a box-lined avenue to arrive at the main courtyard. Who would imagine that a ravishing patio is hidden behind the entrance door framed with camellias and ligularias? Surrounded by a cloister with a vaulted ceiling, punctuated by columns, its monastic charms have been retained. A religious silence reigns in this delightful place, refreshed by a stone pond where Japanese carp swim. "I respected the existing architecture, trimmed the cypresses and olive trees and gave a little helping hand to the wisteria, whose twisted trunk looks like the plaits of a woman's hair. I didn't add anything so as to allow you to feel the emotion which overcame the owners on their first visit here." Once again history is present

as we walk around the house. A large hundred-year-old cypress watches over a stone bench, opposite an octagonal basin. The eye is drawn next to patterns of box, which mark out a graceful web of lines and right angles. "We reconstructed them using the original plans," recalls Jean Mus. "I was very happy to adopt this delicate style and, to link this old garden logically with the terrace of the rear façade, I created geometric motifs in the form of triangles of box surrounded by santolina." This gentle transition leads us to an open space bathed in light. The swimming pool has a minimalist aesthetic, marked in each of the four corners by Anduze vases planted with box, and is echoed by a round stone fountain, its curves in harmony with those of the hills of the Vence countryside. You can find the same refinement, the same elegance in the small *potager* where the owners have planted lemon-colored geraniums, sages, caper shrubs, rosemary, and strawberry trees. However, the garden's most beautiful view has yet to be encountered. Jean Mus created it by taking a stand of gigantic cypresses and transformed it into a grand avenue which descends to a round pond surrounded by laurel trees. Did he base his design on a picture by Hubert Robert? The perspective, drawn with an innate sense of organization, certainly appears to lead one to this conclusion. "This house, built in the spirit of the eighteenth century, required a space which was rather secret and romantic. The trees lent themselves to this interpretation and served as a frame to an idyllic picture, the village of Saint-Paul-de-Vence appears in a faraway blueish haze, shimmering above the pond like a waking dream.

Facing page: Seen from the bottom of the main avenue, the architecture of the steps with their gradations of grass and stone, is punctuated by agaves and a curtain of cypresses.
Above, left: *The monastic sobriety of the cloister has been maintained without interrupting the play of shade and light.*
Above, right: *The lapping of the water in the pool of the fountain barely troubles the silence of the patio.*

Above: Hydrangea quercifolia accompany an Anduze vase to either side of the main door.
Right: Opposite the swimming pool on the hills behind Nice, a rectangular basin forms part of the elegant geometry of the terrace. At the foot of old green oaks, a collection of hardy perennials weaves a disordered carpet, where the yellow of the hemerocallis livens up the greenery.
Facing page, top: The perspective effects in the Mediterranean are magnificent, above all when they are based around a village.
Facing page, bottom: A radical idea, the approach to a wood of green oaks.

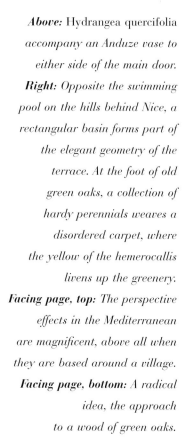

It's magical!" The view of the avenue seen from below is just as attractive. From this perspective you discover stone steps which gently divide the grass slope. Climbing this green staircase, one can inspect the borders and see in close-up the changing colors of the plants: vittadinia, myrcines, and agapanthus. Lined up like statues with sharp claws, the agaves play the starring role. On the right, in the forest of pines and green oaks where little light shines, one can make out a cabin perched atop a large Aleppo pine. "I designed it in partnership with the mistress of the house," says Jean Mus proudly. "Its railing is made of strawberry-tree wood. I gathered all the large branches and cut up the trunks of a few trees which had had to be cut down to construct the cabin. By lining up and stacking these logs, I created my own version of Land Art."

If in principle the cabin is aimed at the owners' children, the area for playing boules, among the most beautiful in Provence, brings together the whole family. Shaded by green oaks, bordered by delicate myrcines and the red foliage of nandinias, this enclosed space marries aesthetics with a sense of fun. And even if you are not skilled in the fine arts of *pétanque*, you can taste all the pleasures of country life and cultivate a lifestyle based on emotions, playing, and sharing.

Stone Steps and Waterfalls

Above: *Original sketch for the water channel and the pool at the foot of the hill on which the* bastide *is built.*
Facing page: *Barry Flanagan's famous hare defies the pretty order of the groundcover plants, among which some superb Geranium tomatosum.*

Perched on the summit of a hill in the countryside near Grasse, a *bastide*, flanked by a small tower topped with a wrought-iron pinnacle, could be the setting for a fairy tale. The owners fell in love with the estate because of its exceptional location and its glorious past. While wishing to pay homage to the history of the Grasse area, which was occupied by the Romans, the owners wanted a well-constructed contemporary garden which took its cue from the uneven contours of the site. "There was only one man who could understand what we wanted and that was Jean Mus," they agree. The house, built on a rock, required a very calculated, premeditated approach, with a certain sense of suspense. Before the property comes into view, you advance slowly along a drive which gently climbs through green oaks before emerging on a plateau at the foot of the hill.

"We find ourselves here on the site of a Roman camp, which is what gives the property its name," explains Jean Mus. "It's a strategically important place because of its dominant position. Over the centuries, the location lost its military purpose to become a farm. So I accentuated this natural evolution by planting olive trees and Provençal cypresses, adding touches of gray and blue by using lavender and rosemary. The architecture of the house, which has elements of Belle Époque style, demanded a more refined approach. I based the overall layout of the garden on a certain geometry of forms, softened by the presence of water. The access paths were lined up with the main axes, and these and the perspectives have been studied in minute detail in order for it to look good in both directions. I had to remodel the hill to achieve this—which was a bold move, but enjoyable."

To integrate the plants with the buildings, Jean Mus used the flexible approach recommended by Russell Page, the British landscape gardener and author of numerous books. In *The Education of a Gardener* he wrote: "To make a garden is to organise all the elements present and add fresh ones, but first of all, I must absorb as

Left: *In front of the guests' house, a trellised vine offers its shade to a wooden bench.*

Facing page, top: *Making a reference to the Moorish patios, the orange trees frame a marble fountain. When in flower their perfume rises to the study of the master of the house.*

Facing page, bottom: *The circle of the pond ends the straight line of the water-staircase, following a geometry which Jean Mus adores.*

Following pages: *Made of small pebbles placed one against the other the Provençal calade is transformed into a waterfall which follows the contours of the hill.*

best I can all that I see, the sky and the skyline, the soil, the colour of the grass and the shape and nature of the trees. Each half-mile of countryside has its own nature and every few yards is a reinterpretation."

With the aim of reconciling the character of the place and his personal inspiration, Jean Mus varied and balanced the moods of the garden according to the demands of the topography. So from the tower, the epitome of a romantic and civilized place, the visitor has a view plunging onto an intimate patio, bordered by box and lemon trees, which protects a cave overrun with vittadinia. The harmony of the whole and the regimentation of the plants are dependent on a focal point. After having traced out the straight lines, Jean Mus drew the curves which start on the upper terraces and continue into the surroundings, using thousands of tons of rock to restructure the landscape.

The straight line of a channel of water divides the hillside, apparently originating under the main terrace. Following an imposing stone staircase bordered by myrtle bushes, polygonum, and rosemary, it flows into a pond, watched over by a malevolent Barry Flanagan statue with its feet among the water lilies. This channel has a number of roles: it is a very useful part of the drainage system in rainy weather, and it also plays a major part in the aesthetics by highlighting the mass of the trees and shrubs and by underlining the dominant position of the house. "I'm delighted by the slightly cheeky contrast between contemporary art and the reminder of a period of history which the layout of the garden brings," interjects Jean Mus. "Because it's impossible not to react when faced with this totally anachronistic

Above, left: *These classic*
compositions have contributed
to the success of Jean Mus's
gardens, reinterpreting,
in his own way, the look
of low-growing vegetation typical
of the Provençal countryside.
Above, left: *In a symphony*
of greens orchestrated
by lentisks and dwarf
pittosporum, terra cotta pots
form part of the architectural
composition.
Facing page: *The gardener's*
house disappears under
a vine behind the dark
silhouette of a cypress.

dialogue." In the sunniest part of the property, which is wide open to the surrounding countryside, the foreground of the garden is therefore incorporated into the topographic forms situated behind them in order to create a coherent composition. The same plan is repeated as you head toward the foot of the hill and prepare to gaze upon the wider landscape. Two spheres of box which frame a fountain on the upper terrace echo the two large plane trees near the swimming pool.

On the lower beds and the rocky outcrops Jean Mus has recreated the "palette garden" beloved of Page, its masses of pastel colors forming a suite of impressionistic compositions. The visitor cannot help but dream of the pastoral scenes of Sisley and Monet. The owners nurture a passion for climbing roses: they have grown Lady Banks and Chinese roses near the summer dining room, which they can admire while sunbathing. In spring, a spectacular collection of eye-catching irises spring forth in front of beds of laurels, blueberries, lavender cottons, and jasmines. Stairs bordered with polygonums snake through the groves, revealing at each turn a charming view built from a hundred-year-old olive tree, a ruined well, or a fountain and leading to a playful and poetic installation of garden gnomes by the contemporary artist, Julie Hayward.

"Since the Roman occupation, several mysteries of this place haven't yet been explained," recounts Jean Mus with a sly smile. "The most recent is the story of the earthworms. A couple of years ago, the owners mail-ordered live earthworms to improve the quality of their compost, but the parcel never arrived. Somewhere in France these earthworms are in the process of multiplying and destroying a post office. We read the papers every day, dreading the outcome of this inevitable catastrophe, but we have made a pact to support each other if the worst happens!"

Facing page: To maintain the link between the house and the countryside, a flight of stone steps follows the steep slope of an area planted with olive trees.
Above, left: The quality of construction of the dry-stone walls is a crucial factor in maintaining a rural architecture which endures through the centuries.
Above, right: In steeply sloping undergrowth, on a carpet of colchia ivy, Acanthus mollis grows tall above the dark leaves of the ligularias.

GARDENS UNDER THE INFLUENCE

The Quinta Garden in Portugal

Preceding pages: A dovecote looks over a garden of box composed in triangles, enclosing a carpet of vittadinia.
Above: Replanted with care, these natural meadows, dotted with olive trees and green oaks, dazzle the visitor with their palette of colors, set off by the leguminous plants (delphiniums, poppies) and the cistus. These require no maintenance whatsoever.
Facing page: Adjacent to the main house, this walled garden shelters four-seasons lemon trees, which enliven the parterres composed of santolinas.

Very near to Evora, the former Roman capital of Portugal and today the capital of Alto Alentejo province, the countryside still shows traces of a brilliant civilization. While the aqueduct, built in the first century C.E., is nothing more than a superb monument, the presence of water is still revered, as it is so rare after the end of spring. From the month of March, the hills are covered in a carpet of flowers and a symphony of greens: "It's a dazzling and moving sight," says Jean Mus, "when you know that in May everything will be burnt up by the sun." Stimulated by the challenge set by nature, whether generous or harsh, he created a collection of gardens which surround a magnificent property, an old fortified farm, commonly called a quinta.

"Don't look for the signs of a nobleman's house here," the owner points out. "The traditional quinta is more closely related to a farm. The landowners and nobility of the region preferred to live in town. Many of them owned palaces in Evora. They took refuge in the countryside in the event of danger and could live self-sufficiently until peace returned. As you know, there were many battles between the Moors and the Christians, and later the Napoleonic invasions."

Surrounded by vines, meadows, and forests of oaks where herds of deer and wild boar live, the quinta stands proud in spite of its great age. Dating from the sixteenth century, its inner courtyard, closed off by a gate decorated with the crests of the owners, is shaded by plane trees in the traditional way and bordered on its perimeter by the main living quarters and the outbuildings. Situated a little higher than the other buildings, a small chapel looks down over the site. Religion plays a part in daily life in Portugal: meadows, vineyards, and woods shelter small altars lovingly maintained by the rural population.

Steeped in the knowledge of the turbulent past of the region, Jean Mus has created a collection of gardens which combine ornamentation and rural productivity. Witnesses to the past, the olive trees and the citrus fruits are treated with infinite respect.

Left: In the middle of the walled garden, circles of dwarf box frame an armillary sphere, used in the past by Portuguese navigators to study the movement of the earth and the stars. The complementary colors of gray and green contribute to a serene spectacle.

Right: Behind the iron gate of the garden, a thoroughbred comes to greet visitors. In a quinta, horses and dogs are never very far away and love to take part in daily life.

"Quinta gardens have always fascinated me, because I could recognize the age-old wisdom of their creators, which is often accompanied by a remarkable sense of beauty. Here in Evora, I envisaged this collection of gardens according to a principle that was both historical and logical—a conversation between the open and the closed." The whole property is articulated around this idea: the heart of the house and the small gardens which frame it are enclosed, intimate spaces governed by feelings of security and abundance. The four enclosures are green rooms, independent one from the other, which serve as additional living rooms and are used depending on the time of day. At sunrise, the patio with the aviary welcomes morning guests. The cooing of doves masks the sound of lapping water in an octagonal pond. In the shade of the large cypresses, a white marble Endymion watches from a distance over the squares of santolina which are organized around a celestial globe. Punctuated by four olive trees and lemon trees, box trimmed into hedges and shaped into spheres sketch out simple geometric forms in this closed, intimate space where you can breath deeply the perfume of flowering citrus trees. Without being asked, Jean Mus confesses: "Perhaps because of the heady fragrances, the use of water, and the stone walls which screen out the world outside, this patio speaks to me of journeys, especially those made by Portuguese navigators to the Indies. I've tried to interpret their memories by bringing together sensuality and refinement." The rose garden that decorates the facade is more exposed and functions as a place of transition and change. The bench which encircles a Japanese privet serves more as a visual aid than as somewhere to sit. With the agreement of the owner, Jean Mus planted in parallel lines hundreds of pale-colored roses—Lady Banks and Iceberg—to celebrate the return of spring with pomp and ceremony. "Here in Portugal," he says, "the delicate and ephemeral beauty of roses seems to me to be more moving than anywhere else. You pause to reflect on and salute this pearly, fragrant miracle which only lasts for the space of a morning." At the back of the house, a swimming pool placed like a precious stone in an emerald-green lawn occupies the third enclosure. A little further on, in the fourth garden

Preceding pages: *Used to store water for the vegetable garden, the large, octagonal pond is surrounded by a splendid rose garden. Composed by an expert hand, bouquets of roses adorn the living rooms and bedrooms of the quinta.*

Above, left: Surrounding a large Japanese privet, a circular bench evokes a recent visit to England.

Above, right: A gazebo overrun with pearl-colored roses overlooks the countryside and the potager.

Facing page, top: In flower for six to eight months a year, the carpet of erigeron strewn with spheres of box shows with its graphic lines the harmony of the wider landscape.

which opens onto the hills, geometry returns. A more elaborate design has been used in this space, which serves as a link between domesticated nature and the wider landscape. Jean Mus chose triangles of box which he filled with vittadinia, making a contrast between the graceful white flowers and the dark green of the shrubs' foliage. The multiple use of the triangular form works well on this more irregular ground, dominated by a wrought-iron arbor overrun by an ancient rose. The hedges become lower, and the openings more frequent, the closer one gets to the exterior of the property. After playing with straight lines, the landscape architect works with curves so that the transition between garden and landscape is made gently. The eye is drawn to a bridge which sits astride a stream full of arum, then upward to find, as if in a painting by Matisse, large planes of bright colors—yellows, violets, and blues. The field of vision, at first narrow and limited, opens out to a wide view of the rolling hills, planted with green oaks, olive trees, and rock roses. A path leads to small lake fringed with yellow water irises and strewn with water lilies. At the edge of the lake, a pontoon has been constructed and a wooden gazebo built, open to the four winds, which can shelter elegant buffets for alfresco meals, bathing parties, or gentle naval jousts.

In this magnificent countryside where nature rules, Jean Mus has made few changes. "I intervened a few times to reframe a landscape from a particular viewpoint, but I never intruded. In fact, while working on the dialogue between the closed and open gardens of the quinta, I have learned a lot, my vision has grown, and my palette of colors has been livened up. The lifestyle of the Alentejo region guided me, and I tried to recreate the harmonious, I might even say, loving dialogue, which has brought together private gardens and an ideal rural retreat."

*Below: Large walnut trees half
hide the white walls of the quinta
in front of a straight avenue
of box. The avenues of schistous
sand are laid out following
a precise and rigorous plan.*

Memories of Italy

Above: *Original preliminary sketch of the project.*
Facing page: *Standing against a low dry-stone wall, bushes of* Echium fastuosum, *whose blue flowers stand up like tufts, celebrate the return of spring.*

A little piece of Tuscany has found its home on the side of one of the numerous hills which overlook the fortified village of Saint-Paul-de-Vence. The owners, in love with Italian culture and Venetian festivals, asked Jean Mus to create a setting worthy of their house, a villa with an ocher facade which seems to have been built according to a design by Palladio. Jean Mus remembered the lessons learned on the job, on the Italian side of the Alps: "The great Roman gardens of the seventeenth century weren't designed to welcome guests for long stays, just for the duration of a party. They needed to offer a brief glimpse of the extraordinary, a moment of enchantment, before disappearing." The difference here is that in a Jean Mus garden, the party must go on forever.

The property lent itself perfectly to this poetic and playful interpretation and fitted the geographical hierarchy recommended by Alberti, the Florentine humanist and architect: "The garden must look down toward the town, the owner's land, the sea, or a great plain." Set down in a landscape of wooded hills which dominate the village of Saint-Paul, the villa is mistress of all she surveys, at the heart of a design orchestrated with a masterly touch by Jean Mus. Extending the rectangular architectural order of the villa, a central driveway crosses the different levels of the garden and imposes a unity on the whole. As in the gardens around Florence, the geometry of forms is evident: axes, perspectives, terraces, balustrades, staircases, gazebos, and fountains heed the demands of a rigorous plan, meticulously designed and implemented. Giving priority to perspective, the planting picks up the rhythm of the lines and volumes according to a logical and consistent continuity. Beds of box, laurels, and spherical or cubic pittosporums outline small green rooms, bordered with rosemary, blue agapanthus, and lavender. The color blue triumphs over the spectrum of greens and echoes the Mediterranean which can be seen in the distance. In high summer, the exuberance of the flowers overpowers the severity of the design and encourages fantasy.

__Left:__ The villa's buttresses jut out into a subtly constructed garden. Geometric forms are balanced by irregular ones, thus dissipating an over-formal rigidity.
__Facing page, top:__ Taking up the axis of Italian-style gardens, Jean Mus brings his poetry and personal imagination, livening up the central stone line with spherical shapes and vegetation.
__Facing page, bottom:__ The grand stairway marks a long oblique line across the hillside, punctuated by olive trees, Convolvulus cneorum, *and* Polygonum capitatum.

Jean Mus recalls, "To communicate the message which the owners had devised, I had to find a harmony between the geometric and very formal, and the bucolic charm of a country garden. The sequence of terraces which is the prerogative of the Italian garden appeared to me like a blessing. The idea of the water channel descending from the villa alongside the two staircases to flow into a pond at the bottom was compelling."

From this central and vertical axis, the garden quickly fell into place. Respecting the symmetry, the order, and the balance of the proportions, the steps which accentuate the landscape mark out the obligatory stops on each terrace by creating strategic viewpoints. The double staircase highlights the theatrical quality of the property and lends itself to all kinds of scenery. The steepness of the slope forces visitors to slow their pace, lending their bearing a kind of majesty which shows the ladies' outfits and the styled elegance of the gentlemen to good effect. Halfway up the path, a swimming pool surrounded by statues invites relaxation, as do the refined surroundings of the gazebo's small salon, painted in the same ocher color as the villa.

Following Italian tradition, the presence of water is vital. Tamed and liberated from gravity, it leaps in waterspouts from the ponds and falls in cascades, illustrating the role of science in the garden, and showing with brilliant mastery the superiority of man over nature, which is nevertheless still present in this imposed order.

"In designing the double staircase," says Jean Mus, "I could already hear the sound of water tumbling from the top of the garden from a fountain which appeared to have its source under the house. The babbling of the water gets louder and stays with you as you move down. It's followed by the bubbling sound of the water in the basins which are laid out along the lower terraces, and finally the murmur of the water as it flows toward the pond at the very foot of the estate. During the hours of

the day when it's burning hot, it's a joyous and refreshing music: once the evening comes it is a little night music which is light and languorous."

To demystify the character of the garden created by the central line of the staircase and the sequence of terraces, the trees and plants celebrate the force and simplicity of the Provençal earth. Hundred-year-old olive trees are planted along the terraces, interspersed with white mulberry trees, magnificent almond trees, and finally fruit trees. "I added some strawberry trees for the taste of their fruit," confides Jean Mus, "because I have memories of tasting the delicate berries at Christmas time."

But the geometry quickly reasserts itself: bordering the terraces, brush and scrub vegetation—thyme, rosemary, lavender, and sweet bay—underscore the horizontal lines which carve out the hillside. Jean Mus adds: "If I lived in the grayness of Paris, I wouldn't stop dreaming about the fragrances which envelop you each step of way. In the South we take a deserved pleasure in small things."

Not so long ago, during a Venetian party and to the sound of violins playing—who else but Vivaldi?—a gondola drifted on the blue waters of the swimming pool, and a farandole of guests in satin cloaks whirled around a pond watched over by large cypresses. Along the main avenues, looking for a potential Casanova, marquises flirt from behind their velvet masks with a harlequin, a priest, a doge, and three gondoliers, without listening to the peals of laughter from a certain Goldoni. In the moonlight and the glow of the torches, masks are followed on by the dance called bergamask, transforming the garden into an enchanted theater.

You might be confused as to whether you are in Tuscany or Venice. It is all a question of lighting. Under the sun, with symmetry and geometry triumphant, the garden is Florentine. At night, it is a Venetian baroque scene that awaits the visitor. When the shadows lengthen and soften the perspective, when the grand statue of Louis Cane is multiplied in the surface of the water and the ponds become magic mirrors, illusion reigns and the party can start at last.

Preceding pages: "This composition, which I have been shaping for thirty years, is in response to the demands of the volumes and colors. Happily, it doesn't require much maintenance. It's up to the gardener to go with the concept from the start, to allow the garden the freedom to express itself." Box, westringia, gray and green santolinas, African boxwood, Tarentina myrtle, and common myrtle are placed like jewels on an irregular checkerboard of Burgundy stone.

Facing page: Flanked by two cypresses, an eighteenth-century fountain in soft stone highlights the nobility of the reception courtyard.

Above, left: An Italian-style vine trellis produces marvelous muscat grapes for eating. Clumps of white immortelles brighten up this scene of greenery.

Above, right: Enveloped by a hedge of Tarentina myrtles, terra-cotta pots contain raphiolepis and punctuate the flank of the hill.

Terraces on the Aegean

A garden is the visual embodiment of the idea of the designer, and to use Marcel Duchamp's phrase, the visual is magical. This garden in the region of Argolis is the ideal embodiment of this formula because it was born from a whim, with the wave of a magic wand. For forty years, a Greek shipping magnate roamed the seas for business and pleasure. However, on board his yacht, he had in his head a constant dream which reconciled his desire to sail the seven seas with his need to return to his roots. A rocky peninsula on the shores of the Aegean Sea awaited him near Mycenae, cradle of one of the most brilliant civilizations of Ancient Greece. A desert site with little attraction but its grandeur offered the possibility of realizing a project dear to his heart: to build a traditional Greek village to bring together children and friends, with houses, small squares, fountains, staircases, and alleyways, and to surround it with a natural landscape imprinted by the hand of man. From his childhood on the island of Andros, the shipping magnate had kept a poetic and radiant vision of the rows of vines and olive trees and the vertical lines of the cypresses which raise their lithe silhouettes above the stocky houses. He also remembered the heady perfume of jasmine and roses. To realize this vivid landscape, he needed a real Mediterranean, a garden specialist with a sensitive soul and an unconditional love for olive trees. He found just such a person in Jean Mus. When Mus disembarked on the peninsula, however, he felt discouraged: vegetation was completely absent, apart from a few sickly shrubs and an immense Aleppo pine, battered by the Meltem wind. The village existed only in a dream. Jean was won over by the contagious enthusiasm of the shipping magnate and started work on his design: each house was different, limewashed, organized around small squares, and built on different levels to take advantage of beautifully framed views of the Mediterranean. Just opposite the "Town Hall," a taverna would take pride of place with a shaded terrace full of rustic tables and chairs. Now all that remained was to transform the heaps of bare rock into gardens of Eden. Through the seasons, tons of earth were

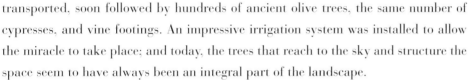

transported, soon followed by hundreds of ancient olive trees, the same number of cypresses, and vine footings. An impressive irrigation system was installed to allow the miracle to take place; and today, the trees that reach to the sky and structure the space seem to have always been an integral part of the landscape.

Arrival at the property is generally by sea. Approaching the private port, an orthodox chapel stands tall above the water between the rocks and the sky, its round roof all in white and surmounted with a cross. The ancients showed their veneration of Poseidon by erecting a temple in a strategic location which served as a landmark for fishermen and seafarers. Over the centuries, the cult linked to the god of the sea was replaced by that of Saint Nicholas, and it is this saint which the shipping magnate, quite logically, has chosen to honor. Climbing the path that leads to the village square, you pass in front of a field of sunflowers whose yellow faces turn insolently toward the changing blues of the sea. There are two paths to choose from, one prickly with agaves which runs alongside a terrace and descends to a beach, the other bordered with a stormy sea of gazanias interspersed with lentisks. A little higher up, fields of lavender, rosemary, and teucrium hug the curves of the site, showing to best effect the symphony of blues and grays beloved of Jean Mus. Further along, behind an enclosure containing a chicken coop and three small donkeys with shaggy coats, the olive trees become denser and share the hill with rows of vines punctuated at each end with rose bushes. Planted according to tradition at six-meter intervals, the olive trees descend lazily toward the sea. As you get closer to the houses, the bucolic landscape takes on a more urban aspect. The garden becomes more civilized around the small square. Like distinguished guests, certain trees are allowed within these privileged limits: mulberry trees, fig trees, pomegranate trees, cypress trees, and three gigantic olive trees which proudly display their symbolic value. A little further on, behind a miniature Garden of the Hesperides and some orange trees with trunks painted white to keep away the insects, stands a majestic Aleppo pine. In this Greek garden, the solitary tree is staged

Facing page: Entirely covered in crazy paving, a traditional technique in the Peloponnese, the small square proudly harbors ancient olive trees.
Above, left: Olive trees frame one of the villas on the property. The olive trees were planted according to the directions of the nurseryman Fostini, who only works in harmony with the moon.
Above, top: The fruits of the pomegranate tree symbolize happiness and fertility.
Above, bottom: Using a mosaic of pebbles common to fishing villages, the steps descend gently to the sea.

Gardens under the Influence

Preceding pages: View of the village built on a rocky peninsula.
Right: *At the foot of a villa renamed "Town Hall," large stone landings allow for the levels to be used for planting, as they hold back the necessary earth.*
Below: *A strategic and convivial meeting place, the taverna overlooks a small, uninhabited island.*

like a hero in a classical tragedy. The Aleppo pine with its imposing bulk dominates a tranquil cove surrounded by white sand. Its emerald-green boughs hide a trunk leaning at a dangerous angle, held up by solid props. The hero is merely wounded. Lower down beside the swimming pool, an enormous dead olive tree with a knotted black trunk seems to claw the horizon. Its monumental size invites comparison with a colossal statue by Henry Moore, incarnating a dream of immortality.

"In every garden, there have to be stars," explains Jean Mus. "Here the trees echo mythology and tell of the loves and hates of Greek men and gods better than any history book. The olive, a tree of peace and glory, is a present from the goddess Pallas Athene to humans. It was with a crown woven from olive boughs that the brows of the Olympic victor were adorned. Straight as a poker, the cypress, associated with cemeteries and mourning, is a tree of life. I could go on—every tree, every shrub has its own language."

Paved with pebbles polished by the sea, the alleyways and staircases cross and recross each other, as if in a labyrinth. Cretan jars, pot bellied and fluted, punctuate the cobbled paths, while bougainvillea, plumbagos, and solanums splash the low walls with flickering flowers of blue and purple. Touches of bright color light up a largely mineral world: impatiens and geraniums spring forth between the paving stones and the oleanders.

Rooted in a land of legends, the Greek garden invites reflection and serenity. It also encourages patience in the face of a nature that has been mastered, but which imposes its rules with as much strength under a burning sun as in the cool shade of the white mulberry trees.

The Belle Époque in Cap Ferrat

At the start of the twentieth century, to own a property on the Cap Ferrat was the privilege of crowned heads, princes of industry and finance, and the great eccentrics. The king of the Belgians at La Leopolda, Baroness Ephrussi de Rothschild at the Villa Île-de-France, the banker and Hellenist Theodore Reinach at Kerylos, the Marnier–Lapostole family at Les Cèdres, Francine Weisweller and Jean Cocteau at Santo-Sospir, and even Somerset Maugham at La Mauresque: each owner rivaled his neighbors in pomp and extravagance, creating extraordinary gardens where audacity and beauty went hand-in-hand. Over the years, through the randomness of real estate transactions and inheritance, the properties have little by little been split up into smaller parcels. More modest in its proportions, the former vegetable garden of the king of Belgium, bought by a Belgian couple, has lost its role as a source of sustenance and become a magnificent flower garden. Familiar with some of Jean Mus's creations, the owners called on him to transform the place. "I immediately understood their need for order and clarity, and I started to design a garden which suited their needs," he recounts while showing round visitors. At first sight, one is seduced by the clean, neatly drawn lines which structure the garden: borders, hedges, groves, and rows of plants trimmed with brilliant mastery. Delicately reinterpreted, the spirit of the Belle Époque still floats from branch to branch and avenue to avenue. Beneath the rose-pink house highlighted with white moldings, Jean Mus has planted buttresses of vegetation, sweet bay trained into a trapezoid shape. At their feet, a lawn of kikuyu—a low-maintenance variety of grass—marks out a rectangle bordered by different sizes of topiary hiding a swimming pool below. But before diving into this aquatic universe, you have to pass under the green roof of a pergola which divides the garden radically with a superb perspective. When the sun is at its zenith, it's a joy to walk under the refreshing arch of a vine. Jean Mus adds in a whisper: "It's a grape that was banned in the past, the

raspberry grape, but I adore its dense, serrated foliage, and the idea of not exactly conforming to the regulations appeals to me."

Another aerial construction, a vine stalk overrun by a wisteria with bunches of mauve flowers, serves as a summer room and a suitable place for meditation. It opens onto a picture of greenery punctuated by topiary, spheres of pittosporum which invite you to climb a flight of stairs made from red bricks. At the very top, an Anduze vase, cypresses, and an olive tree, symbolic emblems of Provence, add their encouragement. Jean Mus smiles: "It's a pointless staircase, it doesn't lead anywhere, but it excites our imagination. Can you read into it a desire for recognition, insatiable desires, professional ambition?" Leaning against the hill, this well-structured garden was created in the manner of a contemporary art installation. Towering over a mass of sphere-shaped vegetation, the verticals of the cypress stand in opposition to the red slant of the terra-cotta steps. On both sides, immortals stand out from the hillside thanks to their elegant gray color. As the pittosporums are happy in their highly protected garden, and to encourage the owners' spirit of collection, Jean Mus happily brought together different varieties: *Pittosporum nana* for the topiary, *P. tobira* and *mannii* for the trees with graceful trunks. An old-fashioned, cradle-shaped bower welcomes bathers in front of the swimming pool. An incurable romantic, the landscape gardener placed a love seat at the heart of profuse vegetation. While relaxing on this rustic seat, one can admire the sculptural forms that enliven a carpet of *Myrsina africana*: topiaried box above which white lantanas and a polygonum with

Preceding pages: In the foreground, a hedge of Tarentina myrtle sits next to spheres of box. Dominated by the massive silhouette of a tall Lambert cypress, the crown of an almost hundred-year-old mandarin tree measures its height against a gazebo, a gracious emblem of nineteenth-century seaside gardens.

Facing page: Playing with forms and shades of green, Jean Mus contrasts the curves and verticals in this romantic composition.

Above, left: Like a green room, this soothing composition highlights an arch of wisteria with blue flowers.

Above, right: Jean Mus has some surprises up his sleeve, punctuating the garden with arbors, permanently decked out in foliage to simulate an eternal springtime.

Gardens under the Influence

Right: This staircase that leads nowhere is a useful prop to suggest depth. The pittosporums are pruned twice a year using secateurs.
Below: Against a backdrop of order, mandarin trees grow and a Tarantina myrtle rests on a carpet of kikuyu.
Facing page: Like a green room, this soothing composition highlights an arch of wisteria with blue flowers.

mauve flowers open out, providing a pleasing contrast to the many tones of green. A hedge of mandarin trees dating from the beginning of the twentieth century runs alongside the swimming pool. Giving rhythm to the space, their trunks are lime-washed and draw the eye to the back of the landscape, where a small gazebo, in virginal white, stands next to four cypresses of royal stature. "This folly, often used in the Belle Époque, fits in with the spirit of the garden," explains Jean Mus. "It is a part of the sentimental architecture that guided the hand of landscape designers at the beginning of the last century. This little pavilion adds an audacious and picturesque touch to a restrained and ordered design." The spirit of the former vegetable garden has not been erased: the cypresses and citrus trees have rediscovered their noble origins, but in place of the rustic beauty of this enclosed garden, another equally delicious history has been substituted, a story which also knows how to speak of happiness with patience and abundance.

INTIMATE GARDENS

A Trompe-l'œil Garden

Preceding pages: Flower-adorned steps connect the main path to the swimming-pool garden. The carefully tended background gives the composition an illusion of depth.

Above: The plan for the radiating pattern of the stones is the main principle behind the execution of this part of the garden.

Facing page: In the foreground, an olive tree looks as though it dominates the scene. It is an optical illusion. Count properly and you will find that this part of the garden only occupies some ten meters.

Scarcely bigger than a pocket handkerchief, this stone-walled, town garden in the center of Cannes comes as a wonderful surprise to the visitor. The owner offered the project to Jean Mus, who had some concerns. He wondered how he was going to create a dream garden which would reflect the owner's sophistication and love of the arts when, as he puts it with a sigh, "there was nothing except a few tired and sorry-looking cypresses." The size of the garden and the owner's express wish for a swimming pool required thought. The solution he came up with was based on the principle of "hiding to reveal." "I applied new rules of perception, based on the limited space, setting, and emotion of the place. And I also liked the fact that man could still find his place in this semi-wild environment, and draw quiet enjoyment from it."

Mus's first task was to divide the garden into two parts, one secret, reserved for the swimming pool, the other more open and designed purely for aesthetic pleasure. Opposite the terrace, a double avenue paved with bricks and separated by an emerald-green lawn leads to the entrance and the garage. Visitors are so enthralled by the plantings, however, that they barely notice this careful composition. Bushes of fragrant osmanthus, gardenias, and laurels grab their attention. To the left, a semi-circle of white stone steps divides an undulating Japanese privet hedge. In front, globes of box and huge olive trees, with flowering lavender beneath, hide the terrace from view. To the right, a hedge of cypresses, overrun with laurels and edged with yellow flowering ligularia, gives protection to a wall fountain. Directly opposite, a stele supporting a stone vase decorated with antique bas-reliefs, hides amid a profusion of shrubs—choisya, osmanthus, and honey-fragranced sarcococca—chosen for their scent, as Mus explains.

Herb-covered, stone steps lead to the other part of the garden. "The subtlety of these plants tones down the whiteness of the stone and emphasizes the near-wild beauty of this well-maintained garden," comments Jean Mus, mindful of the tiniest

detail. An element of exoticism has been introduced to the area around the classically shaped swimming pool. Cycads adorn two corners of this closed garden, but star billing is given to a sweep of cherry laurels and globes of box of all different sizes. A bench beneath an arch of Lady Banks roses is a place to share secrets, while another, brought over from England, sits cloaked in roses and vittadinia. White flowers—rose bushes, lilies, lemon tree, bacopa, osmanthus and jasmines—are given pride of place. The only pink blooms allowed here are those of the headily fragrant datura.

The smaller the garden is, the more attention it requires. A landscape arouses emotion, and to express that one needs to perfect the intimate vision and to treat the space like a series of small paintings, to decide between symmetry and asymmetry, and even to re-orientate a view, if necessary. The geographical limitation of an enclosed area gives emphasis to the design. The undulating shape of the hedge harmonizes with the horizontal and vertical lines, and the plants act as both frame and focal point.

In this Cannes town garden, there is a cursory nod to Japanese garden design, from which Jean Mus has adapted one or two rules in order to maximize the use of space and establish a certain beauty and serenity. "Here, again, you have to prune in order to reveal what's there," he recalls. "Pruning is like recreating something. The bushes here form a very dense and structured landscape across several levels, so by pruning them, I can achieve a sense of depth, and that's very important in this restricted space."

Through clever use of a range of colors and foliage the overall harmony of the garden is powerfully and logically expressed. Here, as in Japan, time is the great architect. With it come knowledge and patience, a cardinal virtue in a gardener.

*Facing page: A fountain nestling in dense vegetation forces the visitor to listen and come closer. Protected by two cypresses, the blooms of the winter-flowering mimosa (*Dealbata*) give a touch of warmth to the January chill.*
Above, left: In an unbelievable five square meters, a composition of green and white conceals the terrace.
Above, right: Agapanthus umbellatus *waits for June before bursting into bloom for at least a month.*

Above, top: In front of the entrance, a single thousand-year-old olive tree provides the owner with all the oil she needs— fifteen liters per year.
*Above, bottom: Japanese bamboo (*Nandina domestica*) is unaffected by the changing seasons. Edged with wonderful, dark-leaved senecios, a path laid with terra-cotta tiles from Salerno leads discreetly to the garage.*
*Right: The illusion is complete alongside the swimming pool. Fig trees bearing succulent fruit (*Ficus carica*) frame a sensual curve of cherry laurels.*

Laurels and Lavenders

Above: Traditional paving design makes unique use of the local limestone.
Facing page: "The method I adopted was to adapt the architecture of the garden to contemporary tastes. These sensuous shapes, made up of Pistacia lentiscus, *prostrate rosemary,* Rosmarinus officinalis, *and* Pittosporum tobira nana, *remain resplendent throughout the year."*

In Valbonne, amid a typically Provençal landscape, a garden which, in the past, followed a rather unimaginative horticultural tradition has become a true reflection of contemporary architecture. Its Dutch owners, who are passionate about art and ecology, asked Jean Mus to create a garden based on the design principles of Piet Mondrian and Frank Lloyd Wright, who wrote, "And at the beginning of structure lies always and everywhere geometry."

Nestled in the countryside, the villa retained its typically Mediterranean look, with its tile roof and wide terraces. It was just the garden that needed reworking. "It was a challenge," explains Jean Mus. "Starting with what was a very Provençal garden, I had to come up with a look that was much more modern, but one that wouldn't destroy the intimate ambience of the place." The entrance to the property attests to the new look. In this garden, however, in contrast to the cubist garden conceived by Gabriel Guévrékian at Hyères for the Villa Noailles, the emphasis is on plants rather than stone structures. Generous rows of topiary of all sizes line the avenues, creating a symphony of greenery. Cypresses and olive trees form handsome, vertical lines beneath which bushes, hand-sculpted with shears and secateurs, appear at an oblique angle. Pittosporum, juniper, rosemary, jasmine, box, lentisk, germander, and convolvulus gather on a carpet of pachysandra. In front of the house, lavenders conceal a parking space and introduce a romantic lounge room, set against a hedge of sweet bay laurel in the welcome shade of a large oak. Treated with respect in this garden, this particular laurel, *Laurus nobilis,* pays tribute to Apollo and brings to mind the ancient ceremony, still performed today, of bestowing the title "laureate" upon the winner and crowning him with a wreath of beautiful green leaves. Jean Mus, ever the refined gourmet, points out a feijoa tree, imported from Argentina, the fruit of which tastes of pear and rose. In the lower garden, however, the best is still to come. Access is by a short path lined with topiary, forming a logical link with the preceding

Right: The roundness of the shrubs is echoed by the vases and the Biot oil jars, and adds softness and sensuality to the entrance of the property. The crazy paving is particularly successful.

*Right: Framing a field of lavender,
tables of* Buxus sempervirens
surround the stone steps.
*Below: The rows of lavender give
this part of the garden a permanent
architecture. The Aleppo pine owes
its common name of "white pine"
to the color of its bark.*

garden. Carefully positioned osmanthus, choysia, and santolinas, their sizes and shades of green at play with each other, are a pleasure to behold.

In the middle of a paved courtyard sits a round pool edged with dwarf box. This courtyard is the main axis from which the rest of the garden is arranged. Lower down, an obelisk is lost in a wall of ivy, while higher up, the villa's terraces are hidden behind olive and citrus trees. The view from the summer dining room is brilliantly orchestrated, allowing the rigorous composition and gracious outlook to be fully appreciated. Drawn by the clear blue waters, one's gaze lingers over the swimming pool. Surrounded by lawn and punctuated by four cypress trees which the owner was adamant he wanted, this simple, rectangular pool overlooks several tables of box which, like steps, punctuate the sloping ground. These box hedges, cleverly broken up to form an avenue laid out at an angle, paint a surprisingly modern picture that the parallel rows of lavender, lower down, develop further. Arranged horizontally, the beautiful white stonework of the low, dry-stone walls lends the design clarity and emphasizes the diagonals formed by the globes of teucrium or the sculptured hedges of *Buxus sempervirens*. The work of Jean Mus reveals a fresh perspective which neither erases nor diminishes the atmosphere of intimacy and well-being so closely associated with a private garden. This recent creation is a good illustration of how a garden with just a restricted number of Mediterranean plants can, through playing with harmony and contrast, become a garden more suited to the modern day. After all, surely the role of a garden, be it modern or classic, is to reinvent a vision of happiness and to elevate the relationship between man and nature?

*Preceding pages: An avenue
of* Cycas revolutas *and
a group of* Yucca elephantipes
*provide the one exotic note in
this garden. "In this way, I can
refer to the acclimatized plants
which are still found on the
Cote d'Azur," remarks Jean Mus.*
*Above: Young green oaks
surrounded by a border
of lavender.*
*Right: When the plans for
a garden are being drawn up,
Jean Mus insists to his team that,
"Even if you make it accessible
and easy to maintain,
you can still create
something with personality."
Here, a pond built using
reclaimed materials acts as
a meeting point on walks.*

A Town Garden

Above: Well-protected from the prevailing winds, the four-seasons lemon tree is resplendent all year round.
Facing page: Beneath a hundred-year-old sweet orange tree, round river pebbles are set edgewise with great care. Covered in the green and velvety moss of a helxine, they form a carpet which is both attractive and pleasant to walk on. Acanthus, ligularia, and aralia enjoy this shady atmosphere.

In the principality of Monaco, discretion is part of the lifestyle. On the Rock, as it is called, where vegetation is sparse and precious, it is difficult to imagine that an oasis of greenery is hidden behind the façade of a particular hotel. And yet.... When the owner of an elegant Monegasque house asked Jean Mus to create a garden in an inner courtyard, it came as a real surprise. The owner, an aesthete and collector of modern art and antiques, wanted to create a link between indoors and outdoors, and to take the elegance of the reception rooms and extend it through the green rooms. "To lay out a garden right in the heart of town is never easy," comments the landscape architect. "I had to be realistic about the constraints placed on us and adapt our plan accordingly. That required twice the imagination. As it happens, I took inspiration from Japanese gardens, which are good at playing tricks with false perspectives to create seductive illusions of depth."

Opening onto the town and the sea, the different stories of the house needed a framework of plants in order to restore calm, freshness, and intimacy, while at the same time making the most of the Mediterranean climate. To give the illusion of more space, Jean Mus divided the garden into three very different spaces.

Parallel to the house, a line of arches punctuates a wall of red brick and defines the first space, a lounge and summer dining room. This room, with its terra-cotta floor giving it the appearance of a cloister, increases the area of the inner lounge and retains its sophisticated ambience. The Louis XV wing chairs are replaced by wrought-iron armchairs, and the old-master paintings give way to white, luminous flowers, geraniums, and hydrangeas. Sitting comfortably, the visitor's attention is drawn, nevertheless, by the partly hidden plants higher up. In a display of skilled stage direction, Jean Mus has prepared a treat for us in the form of a proliferation of plants the likes of which one finds in enclosed gardens. And in a display of musical talent, he has arranged it so that the joyful sound of the fountain invites us toward the moss-covered pebble design. But do not be fooled, the design of this garden is not just about whim

and extravagance. Everything has been designed according to strict rules. After the first, circular fountain, over which a stone statue of a duck stands guard, comes a second, wall fountain, cleverly hidden by a bower covered in vines and roses. A border of box marks the edge of the central area, where a cascade of jasmine and colorful geraniums, bamboo, and a Virginia creeper jostle over the upright walls. Amid this prettily managed jungle, giant ferns and alocasias add an exotic note to this clever, artistic study in green. At the rear of the garden, separated by the wall fountain, two sitting rooms nurture their secrets. One is completely hidden by a giant orange tree, its fruit gleaming like a winter sun. Beneath this acanthus flowers stand proudly. These two boudoirs are invisible from inside the house and allow family and friends to relax in a silence interrupted only by birdsong and the murmur of the fountain. With the red of the bricks and the green of the plants, we are bathed in a Mediterranean atmosphere, making it easy to forget we are in the center of town, close to the prince's palace. As Jean Mus exclaims, "What I like is this romantic chaos which contrasts with Monegasque protocol, which has as many ruled lines as a sheet of music! I hope that the unbridled, sometimes wild, proliferation of plants can act as a catalyst to introduce an element of fun into a way of life that can sometimes be too urban."

Facing page: Rocks and plants fit well together in the heart of this very shady garden. The trunk of an orange tree partly hides a circular basin echoed simultaneously by the curve of the box, itself emphasized by the white cyclamens.
Above, left: To light up this green living room in the heart of town, the owner places candles in old Roman tiles.
Above, center: In this enclosed garden, only shade-loving plants thrive. Among them, Aralia japonica *ferns, phormium, mixed tenax, and helxine.*
Above, right: Inspired by Moorish gardens, a pebble path links the various parts of the garden.

Preceding pages: *From the living room, the view across the three gardens is an almost-perfect symmetrical composition. Behind the central pool, a fountain in the wall is the vanishing point.*
Left: *An arborescent fern spreads its plumed leaves above a bed of ligularia bordered by box.*
Above: *Resting against a wall of the guest house, amid a clever mix of mint geranium and star jasmine, is a Baroque-style fountain, designed by Jean Mus.*

GARDENS OF THE SENSES

A Perfumer's Garden

Preceding pages: Made of specially chosen stones to give the impression of an ancient road, the main avenue is bordered by a succession of perfumed plants, grown in cushion shapes at different heights.
Above: "No," insists Jean Mus, "Vittadina aren't my favorite flowers, although...."
Facing page: A glazed pot seems to spring forth from a clump of dwarf pittosporum at the foot of a summer house. The path which leads to the swimming pool is paved with Estaillade stones.
Following pages: The faïsses *are the walls that hold back the earth, also known as terraces. They represent a universal image of the rural architecture of Provence. In the foreground is an attractive, self-seeded valerian.*

In the hills of Cabris, a garden illustrates the meeting between two Provençals, a perfumer and a landscape gardener. It is a story of good neighbors and also of shared interests, and these have made themselves apparent through the garden. "I have always considered perfumery to be a great art," explains Jean Mus. "When my neighbor, a renowned perfume maker, asked me to restructure his old garden I was very happy. My mission was to develop and exploit the theme of perfume through atmosphere, plants, and structures."

In a dominant position above the bay of Cannes, at an altitude of five hundred meters, this garden benefits from a fairy-tale panoramic view which stretches from Corsica to the Îles du Levant. To show the changing aspects of the Mediterranean at their best, Jean Mus carefully framed the views. The sparkling sea comes into view at a bend in a path, as if by chance through a gap between the cypresses, or appears suddenly opposite the upper terrace. The landscape, whether hidden or revealed by the landscape designer's magic, is not the star, however. It is perfume and its evocation which has guided his design and so this garden represents a landmark in the career of Jean Mus. One enters the property by a long paved avenue, bordered by olive trees and cypresses, the latter used in perfumery for its woody and green notes which lighten men's eaux de toilette. Along a low dry-stone wall, clumps of fragrant plants attract the eye and also the desire to touch: thymes, medicinal rosemary, rock roses, sages, mints, honeysuckles, geraniums, lavenders, verbenas, can be rubbed between hands to awaken the aromas. Opposite the house, Jean Mus has created a waterfall which supplies a fountain nestling in the greenery. The paved path continues to a Provençal *cabanon* or small house, reconstructed from a pile of ruins and open to the countryside of Grasse. In this bucolic setting, in the shade of a gigantic cypress tree, meals are enjoyed all summer long. However, it is in the evening, under the moonlight, that the real charm of the place works its magic. "It's the night jasmine which is responsible," explains the owner. The purple flowers of this shrub,

Right: Near the cabanon, *cushions
of lavender will be used to fill
sachets for perfuming
the cupboards after the harvest,
which takes place at the end of July.*

***Right:** "Our team achieved a remarkable reconstruction of a dry-stone wall by using various sedums and ceteracs," says Jean Mus proudly.*
***Below:** Below the terrace, all the owner's favorite plants give off their heady fragrances (helichrysum, which smells of curry, garum or perfumed geraniums, Arabian jasmines, Spartium junceum, and old-fashioned roses).*

which has many different, evocative names, give off a full and heady perfume, even more intoxicating than ordinary jasmine.

Shaded by hundred-year-old olive trees and bordered by hedges of rosemary, thyme, and santolina which pick up the shades of blue so prized by Jean Mus, the dry-stone terraces descend gently toward the valley, creating a sensual rhythm. "In this garden, it is the fragrances which come to meet you," remarks Jean Mus. The visitor stops to breathe the scent from a jasmine hedge which blocks the path that goes round the house. The swimming pool can be glimpsed briefly, hidden behind the cypresses. Thousands of little white flowers come together to overwhelm the visitor, stopping him in his tracks with their wordless seductions. Visible and invisible, perfume is an architecture, an overwhelming sensation which fills us with pleasure. "Here, jasmine flowers almost all year round," explains the perfume maker. "We harvest it less and less, because it's hard work and has to be done at dawn. The petals are so small and delicate that they need to be picked with little hands; in olden times the work was done by women and children." The smell of roses bursts forth along a narrow flight of stone steps; these seductive plants have not been overlooked. Chinese roses, May roses, Damask roses, Lady Banks roses, all have cheerfully overrun the walls of the house and the trunks of the olive trees. "Don't forget my favorite, the mermaid!" Jean Mus exclaims. "It's a mysterious rose, very feminine, with a stem bristling with thorns. I think that Antoine de Saint-Exupéry used it for inspiration. He remembered its beauty, its perfume, and its impressive thorns when he was writing *The Little Prince* in New York. His mother, who had the house just above this property, loved roses. It was she who taught me to read." And perhaps also how to see with the heart.

Facing page: It is the sense of touch that is highlighted in this composition. The visitor can touch all the sources of perfume. In the foreground, the round fruits of a kumquat, which can be eaten all year round.
Right: "From the terrace you can see Cabris, the beautiful village where I grew up and where I live today," confides Jean Mus.
Below: An American agave adorned with yellow chimera threatens with its prickles a Convolvulus cneorum, which is protecting an ancient olive tree.

A Garden of Perspectives

Certain gardens irresistibly evoke works of art. This property nestling in the hills behind Grasse is a case in point, with its idyllic setting and giant trees recalling the paintings of Jean-Honoré Fragonard, a local boy, just like Jean Mus. In the eighteenth century, just before the upheavals of the Revolution, the idea of nature was of paramount importance as a result of Jean-Jacques Rousseau's novels and the new and growing fashion for English gardens. At the Petit Trianon, in the gardens of the Palace of Versailles, Queen Marie-Antoinette play-acted the role of shepherdess for her amusement and cultivated a new "art de vivre" based on country pleasures. Antoine Watteau, in his "fêtes galantes," painted charming, slightly nostalgic pictures of shady parks which no longer obeyed the cold geometry of Versailles, but celebrated a voluptuous and mysterious poetry. It was in this spirit, at the same time serious and light-hearted, that Jean Mus conceived the garden. He knew the taste of the owners for the Age of Enlightenment and invented for them a garden as fit for reveries of a solitary walker as for masked balls. While the layout of the garden is rigorous and follows the different terraces of the site, it breaks with the idea of the majestic parterre which is inseparable from French-style gardens. In order not to give away everything at first glance, Jean Mus has used many different and surprising effects without forgetting to highlight the remarkable views. The upper terrace is separated by two transverse axes, two stone staircases which divide the area into spaces with different atmospheres and different concepts. Following a logical plan, the garden designed at the foot of the old *bastide*, right under the master's nose, reflects the refined and languid grace of the eighteenth century. A marble statue of two lovers, too well-dressed to be looking after sheep, entwine themselves at the end of an avenue where square beds of box and santolina are interweaved. A bit further along, surrounded by a copse, a green room hides a pool where you can plunge your hands to refresh them. To recreate Fragonard's famous painting one could attach a swing to the branch of one of the big pines or organize a game of blind man's buff. In a spirit

Right: The graceful arcades of an
Italian-inspired pavilion
are reflected in the clear water
of a swimming pool.

__Right:__ The height of plant refinement: the squares of box and santolina occupy the upper part of the terrace, which divides a canal basin.
__Below:__ Punctuated with urns and sculpted stone ornaments, the transverse avenue shows a monochrome collection of Iris germanica.

of curiosity and the desire for other emotions, the visitor descends a flight of stone steps protected by an arbor to reach the lower level. In the spring, the visitor would see only blue, his eyes wandering between the borders of iris and wisteria which tumble down from the pergola in gentle cascades. On the same level, but on the other side of the property, and in a rectilinear alignment, orange trees planted along two avenues are reflected in a rectangular stretch of water, the trees promising fragrance and good food according to the season. As one descends toward the lake which can be found at the foot of the property, each step rejects artificiality. Nature seems to reassert itself, contemptuous of the straight lines that regulate the upper terrace. The Provençal landscape, which began at the top as a path shaded by olive trees bordered by balls of lavender, reappears below the edge of a small lake fringed with reeds where the tree frogs croak their hearts out. Which landscape would you choose? The refined park with the checkerboard pattern of box which serves as a setting for the fleeting shadows of another century, or the bucolic and romantic vision of the hinterlands of Grasse, where disorder, curves, and some unruly plants have taken over?

"The dialogue of contrasts between these two styles corresponds to our own contradictions, to the inconsistencies of our hearts, but it doesn't betray the spirit of the property," asserts Jean Mus. "I think," he continues, quoting Ferdinand Bac, "that one must yield to the panoramic majesty of the place, and that one must adopt an attitude of devotion rather than conquest toward nature." The insertion of a formal

garden into a natural landscape obeys the contours of the site and the history of the property; however, this subtle progression is made using strong, clear lines. Jean Mus remembered the lessons of the landscape designer Russell Page, who at Castel Mougins, orchestrated a grandiose panorama on the crest of a hill. Three ornamental parterres dominate a composition ordered around a central axis—a flight of steps leading down to terraces planted with olive trees and rustic flowers. "But more joyful than the impeccable lines of the garden is the pleasure that it gives you through all the senses," emphasizes Jean Mus. Even without considering the perspectives which delight and fool the eye by abolishing the boundary between illusion and reality, what could be more delicious than the scent of orange blossom, the silky rain of wisteria petals, the music of the wind in the leaves, the taste of water from the fountain? Take care: this garden designed with rigor and finesse is also that of a sensualist, in the strong, noble, and historical sense of the word.

Below: Punctuated by cypresses and white oleanders, the main stairway looks down over the surrounding countryside. At the very bottom, a nobly proportioned marble vase catches the eye.

Preceding pages: Under the protection of a Mediterranean hackberry tree (Celtis australis) ponds of different heights flow into the main canal which surrounds a collection of citrus trees.

A Garden in Perfect Harmony

According to the wishes of the owner, a German industrialist no longer with us today, this garden was created for eternity. How can one apply this difficult, abstract word to a forest of green oaks and pines which covers a hill of about twelve-and-a-half acres near Saint-Paul-de-Vence? Jean Mus thought long and hard about this, juggling with visions of an earthly paradise planted in the hills behind Nice.

"I imagined a dreamlike walk though contrasting atmospheres. There was no question of disfiguring the hill. I had to find the common thread that would link the formal garden and the natural parts. The presence of small valleys and hillsides made breaking up the different landscapes easier. Of course, I thought of the garden that Ferdinand Bac created at Colombières, which paid homage to the multilayered civilization of the Mediterranean coast. I divided the site into three areas and gave each a particular identity, alternating the formal and informal aspects." To the east, near to the main house, the swimming pool is hidden among tropical vegetation, where in summer the flowers are a riot of bright colors. Hibiscus, agapanthus, perovskia, lantana, banana, and palm trees have been planted, treated, as they should be, as "guests." To the west side, the Italian garden hugs the side of the hill with a long rectilinear avenue, paved with stone and punctuated with cypresses. Beginning with a pond under a pergola weighed down with Spanish jasmine, the avenue continues in a marble staircase which leads to a rose-pink temple flanked with cypresses and olive trees and jealously guarded by a strange figure wearing a round hat. To either side, lavenders flower under citrus and hundred-year-old olive trees, each one chosen with care from local tree nurseries.

To the south, breaking up the geometry, is an English-inspired garden where a carpet of thyme and heather stretches out beneath the impassive gaze of two stone lions. Tracing elegant curved lines which follow the contours of the site, Jean Mus has planted multicolored varieties of ground cover, cuphea and nandinas, an ideal but surprising parterre for the date palms and washingtonia, protected in the background

by Aleppo pines and Atlas cedars. "With this part of the garden." he says. "I amused myself with the contrasts and juxtapositions of climates and colors. I wanted solid banks of red and purple broken up with strong verticals, in this instance the trunks of palm trees."

The extent of the garden allowed the designer to make a few innovations. Following one of the paths a croquet lawn appears, which would have delighted Alice and her friends from Wonderland. A bit further on, a path overrun with moss and well-protected by a bamboo plantation leads to a greenhouse, where green fingers are cultivating orchids. While removing the trees from the top of the hill, the team of gardeners found a mass of ruins, which Jean Mus rebuilt into a Saracen tower. These abandoned stones may have been of foreign origin. The valleys of the rivers Loup and Var were guarded by watchtowers which were used for sending messages when the enemy approached—Barbary pirates from the sea. Today, the Stérénal garden tower has no more than a symbolic function, but to add a little mystery to this corner of the garden, and to make the walk more romantic, it is surrounded by a very attractive small maze of yews.

Visible from the house, a wall of water bordered by irises draws the attention of the visitor, its crystalline sounds carried by the breeze. During the summer months, one is irresistibly drawn to the play of light on the cascading water, and by the continuous effects of reflection and transparency which embellish this simple stone wall. This wall of water and sound offers a counterpoint to the music room in the middle of the garden.

A lover of opera and chamber music, the owner wanted to open a clearing in the heart of her garden where she could arrange private concerts. For this space dedicated to music, Jean Mus chose an east–west axis, lit by the rays of the rising and setting sun, and so evoking the theme of the solar cycle and eternity. Framed by imposing Medici vases, a flight of wide stone steps leads to a circular room covered with a lawn, in the image of an ancient theater. A simple stone ledge takes the place of a seat for the music-loving guests. All around, hedges of green oak and Aleppo pines hold back the cool of the evening and form a protective barrier, which also helps the acoustic quality. When the sound of the violins rises to the top of the tall trees, time seems to stand still during a *Lied* by Schubert or a Mozart opera. The music takes over this closed place and enchants it, as if the conductor's baton possessed magic powers. Suddenly metamorphosed by a perfect appropriateness of setting and melody, the garden has finally found its vocation.

Jean Mus intervenes on this point: " Even when there is no musician, the whole garden is a hymn to the joy of living. You have to know how to listen: to the music of the water you have to add the rustling of the leaves and the song of the birds. Nightingales nest in the forest, but only sing at night. In the evening, when the cicadas fall silent, the choir of tree frogs resume their favorite song. It is, in my opinion, this harmony between landscape and music that speaks most strongly of eternity."

Facing page, top: In the month of June, the old formula that brings together hemerocallis and perovskia is always successful.
Facing page, bottom: The wall of water is placed next to a forest of Chinese bamboo. The irises in the foreground protect passers-by from getting splashed by the waterfall.
Above: Around the irregular-shaped swimming pool, date palms and hemerocallis constitute an exotic decor, under the constant influence of perovskia.

Rhythms and Shapes in the Garden

Above: Positioned as a flat area of color, a field of lavender shares a gentle slope with a meadow.
Facing page: As gentle to touch as to look at, the cushions of box and santolina play with the light softened by the branches of a Pichouline olive tree. The pleasing roundness of an oil jar highlights the down and upstrokes with which the garden is drawn.

Around Saint-Paul-de-Vence, each hill lends itself to new scenery and tells new stories. The uneven terrain of the area and the slopes did not alarm Jean Mus, who, with this project, has realized one of his most beautiful creations. Of British origin, the owners called on him to create a dream garden which would serve as a backdrop to an important collection of contemporary art and would reflect their unbridled love for jazz, a passion shared by Jean Mus, who sings blues and ragtime whenever he gets the chance. "From the outset there was a great affinity between us, and I appreciated the free hand that they gave me," comments Jean Mus.

Nothing is more daunting than resolving the problem of access for motor vehicles to a property. It is essential that a wide tarmac road lead to the front door and then quickly lead on to a carefully concealed parking lot. Here, the road winds along the slope, which allowed Jean Mus to create two different pictures depending on whether one is going up or down the hill. Contrasting with the arid road below, an impression of coolness from the undergrowth welcomes you as soon as the main gate opens. A cypress hedge punctuated with olive trees invites you to enter a radically different world where beauty takes center stage. Straightaway, the statues and the contemporary art installations draw your gaze, but after a well-designed corner which hid the rest of the landscape from you, you find yourself in a courtyard of plane trees which precedes the villa's entrance, guarded by two cypress tress. The civilized atmosphere is refined with borders of box and santolina, but this dialogue between two shades of green is interrupted by the sunny colors of lantanas and the deep blue of the astonishing *Plumbagos wilmotti*.

Located on the same level as the elegant house restored by Robert Dallas, the swimming pool seems to flow into the Mediterranean. It is surrounded by sculptures: a winged griffin which is keeping a close eye on a witch by the French artist Louis Cane. Jean Mus interjects in his capacity as a well-informed musicologist: "If one had

to compare this place to a jazz score, it would be a Louis Armstrong trumpet solo, because it's a place filled with sunshine, it gives life momentum, it dazzles with light." The walk continues in the shade of the big plane trees, with just enough time to see a wall of bougainvilleas and rosebushes pruned in waves before a surprise. A secret garden offers an intimate scene where, in front of a wooden bench, a pond is laid out in a semi-circle, in the middle of a carpet of strawberry plants and helxine. "When I am sitting on this bench and hear the murmur of the fountain, I think of Errol Garner's wonderful piano playing," remarks Jean Mus.

The reflection on the theme of the circle continues beyond an arch formed by two cypresses, with another green room set off by the inclusion of red chairs. Pittosporums, perfectly trimmed into spheres, rise up the slope in tiers to form a background to this avant-garde installation. "As a Provençal, I took great pleasure in teaching the owner, in a foreign language, the art of pruning shrubs," says the architect proudly as he continues the walk. A group of figures recalling the majesty of Etruscan statues has taken refuge lower down, near a waterfall which tumbles noisily down the hillside—perhaps like an Eric Clapton guitar solo. To liven up the landscape, Jean Mus simply created a stream which crosses a bed of euphorbia, arums, ligularias, and ferns. Then a curtain of cypresses divides the hill, capturing our attention and acting as a screen for a sculpture by Bernar Venet. A lawn scattered with clumps of lavender leads us back to the entrance to the property, hidden behind a bamboo grove, and we have completed the tour. Near the gate, a sculpture with sharp edges and syncopated lines attracts our gaze.

As in a jazz orchestra, the whole garden takes part in its creation, following a rhythm in harmony. The musical theme is taken up by the instruments each with their own personal improvisation which ends by returning to the melody. "This garden brings joy to the heart, and its analogy with jazz expresses itself in its dynamism and its openness to the artistic world," emphasizes Jean Mus, who shares with Henri Matisse this novel interpretation based on the complicity between music and strong images with dazzling forms and colors.

Facing page: Guarded by enigmatic figures, the waterfall designed by Jean Mus rescues the steeply sloping site. The rocks were found on the property and were positioned with the aim of making them look natural and authentic.

Above, left: Imported from England, the master of the house's bench seems to offer lessons in wisdom.

Above, right: Two bright red chairs light up the undergrowth, adding a stimulating surrealistic touch.

Following pages: Framed by gaura and convolvulus, a country living room brings the owners together around a pond adorned with an imposing contemporary sculpture.

Above, top: "I created surprise effects," says Jean Mus, "by making the avenues follow a winding path which I bordered with agapanthus."

Above, bottom: "We used the leaning trunk of the green oaks to frame intimate and romantic scenes."

Right: On a carpet of lavender in the lower part of the property, a bronze spiral by Bernar Venet contrasts with the vertical lines of the cypresses.

Useful Addresses

UK

Architectural Plants
Cooks Farm
Nuthurst
Horsham
West Sussex, RH13 6LH
Tel: 01403 891 772
Fax: 01403 891 056
Suppliers of big hardy plants, exotics, bamboos, bananas, palms, ferns and evergreen trees.

Society of Garden Designers
Katepura House
Ashfield Park Avenue
Ross-on-Wye
Herefordshire, HR9 5AX
Tel: 01989 566695
Fax: 01989 567676
Email: info@sgd.org.uk
Website: www.sgd.org.uk
Professional association that can give recommendations of suitable garden designers nationwide.

The Mediterranean Garden Society
www.mediterraneangardensociety.org
An international forum devoted to furthering knowledge and appreciation of plants and gardens suited to the mediterranean climate regions of the world. Branches in Europe, Australia, the United States and elsewhere.

UNITED STATES

California Flora Nursery
P.O. Box 3, Somers & D Streets
Fulton, CA 95439
Tel: (707) 528 8813
www.calfloranursery.com
Wholesale and retail, native and Mediterranean plants.

Native Sons, Inc.
379 W. El Campo Rd.
Arroyo Grande, Ca 93420
Tel: (805) 481 5996
Fax: (805) 489 1991
email: native.son@nativeson.com
website: www.nativeson.com
Nursery specializing in Mediterranean-style perennials, grasses, and shrubs.

Sierra Azul Nursery & Gardens
2660 East Lake Avenue (Highway 152)
Watsonville, CA 95076
Tel: (831) 763 0939
www.sierraazul.com
Retail plant nursery specializing in Mediterranean plants from around the world.

Strybing Arboretum & Botanical Gardens
Golden Gate Park
North Avenue at Lincoln Way
San Francisco, CA 94122

(415) 661 1316
www.strybing.org
A public garden with diverse collections of plants from around the world, including Mediterranean plants.

AUSTRALIA

Petals and Buds
Kapunda Road
Eudunda, South Australia 5374
Email: petalsandbuds@hotmail.com.au
Phone: (08) 85811882
Fax: (08) 85811882
Nursery with many Mediterranean-climate-flowering perennials & shrubs.

Seedcentre
Email: info@seedcentre.com.au
Website: www.seedcentre.com.au
Online seed and garden retailer.

www.au.gardenweb.com
Listings of garden-related companies and societies throughout Australia.

www.global-garden.com.au
Free national gardening magazine on the Internet.

Original sketch for La Fiorentina. The pergolas are installed on the highest points, to allow views across the rest of the garden.

Acknowledgments

Jean Mus:
The creation of gardens often leaves a hint of perfume and a feeling of light hanging in the air, which I share, as always, with all my colleagues. They have accompanied me in all areas of my work, allowing our collaboration to mature as much in wisdom as in discovery. It is as a friend that I would like to thank in particular Jean-Jacques Piasco, who has shared all the encounters and emotions of this fabulous adventure from the beginning. Thanks are due to my daughter Florence, who has been working with me for a number of years, and who looks after and inspires the dynamism of our whole team. I would like to thank Jacques Chibois for his shared taste in food and all the gardeners who ensure the longevity of my gardens: Pascal Mermillod, Alexis Caillet, Patrick Chaix, Laurent Toutain, Olivier Trassaert, Nicolas Esclapez, Stéphane Rossi, Pascal Beaumont, Paul Dunan, Anita Morf, Fostini from the Peloponnese. I am also grateful to the owners of the gardens featured in this book, as well as all those who have allowed me to realize a childhood dream.

Dane McDowell would like to thank Jean Mus for having shown her such wonderful properties. She would also like to express her gratitude to Ghislaine Bavoillot, Nathalie Démoulin, Sylvie Ramaut, and Aurélie Sallandrouze for their professionalism and their patience at all times.

Editorial Director: Ghislaine Bavoillot
Art Director and Graphic Design:
Karen Bowen
Translated from the French by
Simon Gwynn
Copyediting: Philippa Hurd
Proofreading: Mark Hutchinson
Typesetting: Thomas Gravemaker

Distributed in North America by
Rizzoli International Publications, Inc.

Originally published in French as
Jardins Secrets de Méditerranée
© Éditions Flammarion, 2005
English-language edition
© Éditions Flammarion, 2006

FC0512-06-III
ISBN-10: 2-0803-0512-3
ISBN-13: 978280305121
Dépôt légal: 03/2006

Color Separation: Penez Édition
Printed in France by Pollina - n° L99032